The Solomon Goldman Lectures

Volume V

Edited by
Byron L. Sherwin and Michael Carasik

The Spertus College of Judaica Press
Chicago, Illinois

5750

1990

Copyright ©1990 Spertus College of Judaica Press
International Standard Book Number: 0-935982-41-8
International Standard Serial Number: 0196-2183
Library of Congress Number: 82-642856

Contents

Editor's Preface	iv
1. **From Sacrifice to Symbol—and Beyond** Baruch M. Bokser	1
2. **Islam and the Jews: Myth, Counter-Myth, History** Mark R. Cohen	20
3. **The "Soules Language" in the Song of Songs** Michael V. Fox	33
4. **Attitudes of the Kabbalists and Hasidim Towards Maimonides** Louis Jacobs	45
5. **The Place of Ethics in Medieval Jewish Philosophy—The Case of Saadia Gaon** Menachem Kellner	56
6. **Diplomatically Speaking: A Language Called "Ladino"** Nancy Kobrin	71
7. **Nahmanides'** *Commentary on the Torah* David Novak	87
8. **Gersonides' Place in the History of Philosophy** Norbert Samuelson	105
9. **Foundations of Jewish Ethics** Walter S. Wurzburger	119

Editor's Preface

Five years have elapsed since the publication of the previous volume in this series. The nine essays that comprise this book are based upon lectures delivered at Spertus College of Judaica as part of its Solomon Goldman Lecture Series from Fall 1984 through Spring 1989. Additional essays based upon lectures given during those years, but received too late for inclusion in the present volume, will be published in Volume Six of the series.

The essays that follow are listed alphabetically by the surname of the author rather than in the chronological order in which they were given in the Solomon Goldman Lecture Series.

In the first essay, by Baruch Bokser of the Jewish Theological Seminary of America, an investigation of the transition of the Passover celebration from sacrifice to symbol, from a biblical festival to a rabbinic observance, is offered. This essay should be read together with Bokser's other groundbreaking research in the study of the development of Jewish religious observance in general, and of Passover in particular. As the Passover Seder is certainly one of the most popularly observed Jewish religious practices, this study will not only be of profound interest to scholars, but will also be pertinent to laypersons seeking to infuse their family Passover observances with deeper meaning and understanding. Bokser's contribution to this volume is based upon a lecture delivered on April 13, 1986.

The complex and volatile situation in the Middle East requires sober scholarly investigation into the historical relationship between Judaism and Islam, and between Jews and Moslems. In his contribution to this volume, based upon a lecture given on May 19, 1985, Mark Cohen of Princeton University offers a fresh and compelling look at popular and scholarly perspectives of these relationships, and attempts to set aright the historical record regarding these crucial historical and contemporary issues.

The blatantly erotic nature of the Song of Songs led the talmudic rabbis to consider removing it from the biblical canon. Reinterpreting the Song of Songs as an allegorical love poem about God, the lover, and Israel, his beloved, convinced them to retain this beautiful book as part of the Holy Scriptures. In his essay, Michael Fox of the University of Wisconsin at Madison probes the original literary content and style of the Song of Songs as a love poem. His penetrating study opens new vistas for the appreciation of this gem of biblical literature. Based upon a lecture delivered on October 13, 1984, this paper will be of interest to all who labor to understand and to be inspired by the depth of wisdom and experience implanted within the biblical text.

In 1985, a plethora of studies, books and monographs were composed upon the 850th anniversary of Moses Maimonides' birth. Despite the enormous wealth of scholarly work on this giant of the Jewish philosophical and legal tradition, much still remains to be done. Once again demonstrating the extraordinary erudition and clarity that have been characteristic of his scholarly work over a long period, Louis Jacobs of London, England, sets forth to present and analyze how Maimonides' thought was evaluated by the kabbalistic and East European Hasidic traditions. Jacobs' lecture, delivered on October 27, 1985, is discussed on page 247 of his autobiography, *Helping With Inquiries*, published in England in 1989 by Vallentine, Mitchell.

While Maimonides was undoubtedly the greatest medieval Jewish philosopher, Saadia Gaon was the "father" of medieval Jewish philosophy. In his study of Saadia's views on ethics, Menachem Kellner of Haifa University presents Saadia as a "case-study," in order to depict the relationship of Jewish philosophy to Jewish ethics. Rejecting views of other contemporary scholars who perceive Jewish ethics and philosophy as being discontinuous with traditional concerns and commitments, Kellner demonstrates how ethics and philosophy are part and parcel of the total organic structure of Jewish tradition. Kellner's lecture, upon which this essay is based, was given on December 6, 1987.

Much attention has been given to the "Jewish" language, that is, Yiddish. However, increasing interest is being expressed in other Jewish languages, especially Ladino. In an essay based upon a lecture delivered on March 18, 1986, Nancy Kobrin of the University of Minnesota explores the nature, development and political implications of the Jewish language of the Sephardic Jews—Ladino. This essay might be compared with Herbert Paper's "The History of the Yiddish Language," in Volume IV of *The Solomon Goldman Lectures*.

Nahmanides' *Commentary on the Torah* is one of the standard traditional commentaries on the central literature of Judaism—the Torah. In his study of this crucial work, David Novak of the University of Virginia demonstrates why Nahmanides' commentary should be included in any listing of "Great Jewish Books." Novak further portrays the nature, concerns and methods of textual analysis that characterize this work. In his last contribution to this series (Vol. I, 11-31), Novak discussed "Law and Ethics in Maimonides' Philosophy." Turning now from the "Rambam" (Maimonides) to the "Ramban" (Nahmanides), Novak continues his characteristically insightful and illuminating investigation of classical Jewish thought.

Nahmanides' most illustrious descendant was Levi ben Gershon (Gersonides). A prolific and innovative philosopher and scientist, Gersonides had a profound impact on the future of Jewish and general European philosophy. In his essay, based upon a lecture given on December 4, 1988, Norbert Samuelson of Temple University shares insights culled from his intensive research on Gersonides' thought. In celebration of the 700th anniversary of Gersonides' birth in 1288, Samuelson offers an appreciation of Gersonides' place in the history of philosophical speculation and focuses on a number of areas central to Gersonides' thought. Samuelson's last contribution to this series, "Causation and Choice in the Philosophy of Ibn Daud," (Vol. II, 81-90), offers a further elucidating glimpse into the perplexities of medieval Jewish philosophy.

The Solomon Goldman Lectures

In the final essay, based upon a lecture delivered on November 16, 1986, Walter Wurzburger of Yeshiva University discusses the nature of Jewish ethics. With deft analysis, coupled with his usual erudition, Wurzburger formulates a basis for Jewish ethical discourse that differentiates it from that of secular philosophy, but which integrates it within classical Jewish theological and halakhic categories of thought.

A final word ought to be offered in gratitude. Spertus College is continually grateful to Rose and Sidney Shure for their ongoing support of the Solomon Goldman Lecture Series. To Dr. Nathaniel Stampfer, Dean and Vice-President for Academic Affairs Emeritus, I am grateful for his many efforts in editing the earlier volumes in this series. To my co-editor, Michael Carasik, my thanks for his hard work, his felicitous frame of mind during an often tedious task, and his thoughtful insights regarding editorial and other technical matters related to the production of this volume. For reasons of reading facility, all diacritical markings have been eliminated in the text. The method of Hebrew transliteration employed here is the editors', utilized for simplicity and clarity. Finally, I am grateful to the contributing authors for allowing us to disseminate the fruits of their scholarship to a wider public.

Byron L. Sherwin
Thanksgiving, 1989
Chicago, Illinois

From Sacrifice to Symbol—and Beyond
by
Baruch M. Bokser

How did the biblical passover sacrifice become represented in the seder by a symbolic substitute? Since this transformation came about as a result of a series of changes in the ritual, to answer this question we must review three stages in the history of the Passover festival and observe several different patterns of religious development.[1]

I

We first turn to the places in Scripture where the passover sacrifice forms the essential element of the Festival of the Passover Offering, which ushered in the seven-day Festival of Unleavened Bread. Exodus 12 presents the fullest biblical account of the evening celebration, setting out what should be done on that first night and how it should be remembered in subsequent years. After bringing a passover sacrifice on the fourteenth of Nisan, the Israelites, in familial groups during the evening, are to eat it with bitter herbs and unleavened bread, and to put some of its blood on the doorposts so as to provide a sign that the Destroyer or angel of death should "skip over" the Israelite homes and afflict only the Egyptian firstborn. The Bible uses the pedagogic device of instructions to a child: "And when your children ask you, 'What do you mean by this rite?' you shall say, 'It is the passover sacrifice to the LORD, because He passed over the houses of the Israelites in Egypt when He smote the Egyptians, but saved our houses'" (Exod. 12:26-27). The sacrifice and placing of the blood are assumed to elicit this question.[2] Since the sacrifice is essential for the protection of the Israelites, it has been seen by many as an apotropaic device, warding off danger.[3] The offering therefore represents God's saving act rendering judgment against the Egyptian gods (Exod. 12:12) and protecting the Israelites. Hence, by the annual act of bringing a lamb on the fourteenth of Nisan and eating it in familial groups, Israelites, instead of imitating the Israelites in Egypt, who would have anxiously awaited redemption, can celebrate the fact of redemption.

All other biblical references to the evening rite likewise attest to the centrality of the sacrifice. Thus Numbers 9:1-14 treats the need for a "second passover" for those who cannot observe the first because they are in a state of ritual impurity or on a journey. They are to bring a paschal offering one month later, and are to eat it with unleavened bread and bitter herbs. The implication is that the holiday cannot be celebrated without the lamb. Deuteronomy 16:1-8, locating the Passover rite in the sanctuary that "God will choose," changes the character of the celebration. This text turns a domestic event into part of a national gathering—though families might celebrate individually in that central location. It further associates with the offering the act of the exodus itself: "Observe the month of Abib and offer a passover sacrifice to the LORD your God, for it was in the month of Abib, at night, that the LORD your God freed you from Egypt." Here too the unleavened bread and bitter herbs are to be eaten with the animal.

The same basic pattern is found in the remaining biblical accounts. In Joshua 5:10-12's description of the first Passover on the western side of the Jordan River, the text mentions the cessation of manna, after which the land provided the Israelites with bountiful produce. Hence eating of the land's bounty may have been associated with offering the passover sacrifice and eating unleavened bread. In 2 Kings 23:21-23 and Ezekiel 45:21 as well, the sacrifice is central. In Ezra 6:19-22, the inherently national and celebratory character of the holiday becomes evident. The Festivals of the Passover Offering and of the Unleavened Bread occur as part of a national celebration at the dedication of the reconstructed Temple. Especially notable are 2 Chronicles 30:1-27 and 35:1-19, which emphasize the great rejoicing and the role of Levites and other experts in singing praises to God, and which specify that the eating of the passover sacrifice took place in kinship groups. Passover, associated with joyous festivity, had thus taken on the dimension of a national holiday. In contrast to other biblical sacrifices, however, all Israelites could take part equally in this offering, and only some of its blood, but not its flesh, would be offered on the altar. This greater involvement served to reinforce the significance of the offering for every Israelite, reminding each one of the Exodus experience.

The postbiblical supplements to the biblical heritage maintain the centrality of the communal sacrificial meal. Jubilees (2nd century B.C.E.) chapter 49, omitting the bitter herbs and referring to unleavened bread only as part of the seven-day injunction, speaks of observing the rite of the passover offering at the central sanctuary and emphasizes the slaughter of the sacrifice and the people's joy as they eat, drink wine (here required for the first time), and praise God. Perhaps echoing Exodus 12's attribution of a protective dimension to the offering, Jubilees further asserts that those who observe the Passover will be free from plague in the coming year; it thus applies the message of Passover to the people's future in terms other than those of national independence. The epic Greek-Jewish poet Ezekiel (2nd century B.C.E.), sources from the Jewish community in Elephantine, Egypt (5th century B.C.E.), the practices of the Samaritans, and the Temple and Qumran Scrolls likewise refer to an evening celebration only around the sacrifice. The Wisdom of Solomon (written ca. 37-41 C.E.) 18:2-25 adds to the meal the custom of praising God, also reflected in the first-century authors Philo and Josephus.

Philo and Josephus, otherwise closely following the biblical record, speak of the celebratory nature of Passover as a national thanksgiving for the deliverance from Egypt and describe the multitude of participants who came on pilgrimage to Jerusalem, the great number of sacrifices eaten in kinship groups, and the singing of the Levites, accompanied by musical instruments.[4] Note how Philo, who writes as if from the start the passover sacrifice had been offered as an act of appreciation, associates the celebration with the action of bringing the sacrifice:

> In this festival many myriads of victims from noon till eventide are offered by the whole people, old and young alike, raised for that day to the dignity of the priesthood. For at other times the priests according to the ordinance of the law carry out both the public sacrifices and those offered by private individuals. But on this occasion the whole nation performs the sacred rites and acts as priest with pure hands and complete immunity. The reason for this is as follows: the festival is a reminder and thank-offering for that great migration from Egypt which was made by more than two million of men and women in obedience to the oracles vouchsafed to them.... So exceedingly joyful were they that in their vast enthusiasm and impatient eagerness, they naturally sacrificed without waiting for their priest. This practice, which on that occasion was the result of a spontaneous and instinctive action, was sanctioned by the law once in every year to remind them of their duty of thanksgiving.[5]
>
> (Philo, *Special Laws*, 2:145-146)

Philo's explanatory comment on Numbers 9's "second passover" provides an especially interesting reflection on the diaspora perspective, and again reflects the assumption that without the sacrifice no evening celebration would take place:

> The same permission also must be given to those who are prevented from joining the whole nation in worship not by mourning but by absence in a distant country. For settlers abroad and inhabitants of other regions are not wrongdoers who deserve to be deprived of equal privileges, particularly if the nation has grown so populous that a single country cannot contain it, and has sent out colonies in all directions.
> (Philo, *Moses*, 2:232-233, 6:564-565)

This passage strikingly reflects the crucial role of the sacrifice. There is no extant evidence testifying or even alluding to a nonsacrificial evening celebration. Since the new features in the evening rite found in pre-rabbinic accounts also center on the sacrifice, we must therefore be dealing with a distinct *holiday of the Passover Offering*. Bringing and preparing that offering led up to the experience of the sacrifice, which culminated in the sacrificial meal.

In asserting the essential quality of the passover offering, we cannot deny that some Israelites or Jews who could not offer the paschal lamb may have assumed that they could still participate in the festival. Conceivably, Jews who did not travel to Jerusalem might have wanted to gather without the sacrifice. But the evidence suggests that such a gathering would not have been perceived as the primary means of marking the evening *and by definition would not have been part of the Festival of the Passover Offering*. These Jews could, of course, still observe the seven-day Festival of Unleavened Bread by avoiding leaven;[6] on their own they might gather to usher in the holiday with a special meal, instruct a child on the meaning of the event, offer praises to God, and drink wine.[7] But all those who had once gone on pilgrimage would have realized that they were missing the national celebration. Building on anthropological insights offered by Victor Turner,[8] we can understand how the heightened experience of departing from home and normal social structures, and going on pilgrimage amidst the throngs of pilgrims, would cause people to abandon their usual approach to the world and open themselves to new experiences, in this case a communal experience of the sacred. These diverse pre-rabbinic sources, though they differ slightly in their portrayal of the function of the sacrifice, share in emphasizing its central role. Asking what would happen to the sacrifice once Jews could no longer bring it after the loss of the Temple in Jerusalem in 70 C.E., we come to the second chapter of our story.

II

To the Jerusalem Temple's destruction in 70 C.E. and its attendant religious and communal problems, Jews responded in several different fashions. While we lack evidence regarding the majority of the populace, we do hear voices from several quarters. Some apparently were overcome by their grief at the physical and psychological loss. Others, including those who joined the nascent rabbinic movement, found amidst their grief the means to continue Jewish life.

We can discern two different approaches from amongst the latter. The first entailed imitating the lost sacrifice, which could not be slaughtered, and the blood of which could not be sprinkled on the Temple altar. Gradually this approach was overshadowed by a process of restructuring the celebration. This latter solution both made other religious rituals independent of the cult and drew on and elevated the importance of those biblical rites which from the outset did not require sacrifices. Let us examine how both of these approaches treated the paschal lamb.

At the Temple's destruction, some Jews, apparently not exclusively rabbis, took up the first approach. They prepared a lamb in imitation of the passover lamb—that is, they prepared it roasted whole, in the manner that Exodus 12:9 prescribes for the offering, but would eat it in a family setting outside the cultic area. They would make believe—so to say—that they were having the sacrificial meal. This approach did not become popular among the rabbis, and when the attempt at restructuring the rite gained dominance, the rabbis discouraged imitation. In the following quotation, Rabban Gamaliel and sages reportedly differed over this practice:

> Moreover [in addition to Rabban Gamaliel's three stringencies set out in *M. Beitzah* 2:6] he said three things to be lenient: ... (3) they prepare on the nights of Passover a kid roasted whole [*gedi mequlas*] [in the manner prescribed for the passover offering in Exod. 12:9].
> And Sages forbid [these actions].
>   (*M. Beitzah* 2:7 = *M. Eduyot* 3:11)

The Tosefta analogue to *M. Beitzah* 2:7 provides a definition (A-C) of the "kid roasted whole" mentioned in the Mishnah, and support (E) for Gamaliel's position, but also a challenge from other circles (F-G) discounting that support:

> [A] What is a *gedi mequlas*?
> [B] Completely roasted, [with] its head, legs, and entrails.
> [C] [If] he boiled any part of it, steamed any part of it—this is not a kid roasted whole.
> [D] They prepare a kid roasted whole [*gedi mequlas*] on [even the night of] the first day of the Festival [Sukkot] and on [even the night of] the last day of Passover;
> they prepare a calf roasted whole [*egel mequlas*] on [even the night of] the first day of Passover but not a kid roasted whole [*gedi mequlas*]. [Because the calf never served as a passover offering, using the calf would not represent an act imitative of the sacrifice. Similarly, because the passover offering was eaten Passover night, eating it roasted whole

(*mequlas*) at other times, when there is no synchronization with the passover offering, would be unobjectionable.]
[E] Said Rabbi Yose, Todos of Rome directed [*hinhig et*] the Romans to take lambs [*tela'im*] on the nights of Passover, and they prepare them roasted whole.
[F] They said to him, he in turn [thus] nearly causes them to eat holy things outside [the holy precincts],
[G] because they [the Roman Jews] call them [the lambs] *pesahim*.
(*T. Yom Tov [=Beitzah]* 2:15, pp. 290-291, lines 56-62)

Yose, an early second-century master, in E offers evidence for a position that differs with D's prohibition of a kid roasted whole on Passover evening. Since Gamaliel in *M. Beitzah* 2:7 teaches that one may prepare a *gedi mequlas*, E in effect adduces in the practice of Roman Jews a precedent for Gamaliel. In using Todos as the example, it depicts him as a leader who had an impact on the ritual life of Roman Jews. Since he lacks the title Rabbi and is placed in Rome, we should, however, assume that he was not a member of the rabbinic group. F-G, by referring to the established rule that prohibits eating holy things outside the holy precincts, rejects the precedent of Roman Jewry as inappropriate.[9] Although Mishnah and Tosefta *Beitzah* acknowledge the existence of the practice of imitative substitutions for the lamb, they both play it down. *M. Beitzah* does so by labelling Gamaliel's disputant "sages." *T. Yom Tov* does so by claiming that Gamaliel's option is religiously counter-productive or dangerous. But other sources elsewhere refer to people following that practice, and a text such as *M. Pesahim* 7:2 reports that Gamaliel himself had a kid roasted whole prepared at most only slightly at variance from the standard *mequlas* method:

They do not roast the passover lamb on a [metal] spit or on a grill. Rabbi Zadok says, A case concerning Rabban Gamaliel, who said to Tabi his servant, "Go and roast the passover lamb for us on the grill."
(*M. Pesahim* 7:2)

In light of such sources, we can understand that Yose in the Tosefta may indeed have believed that Todos's actions and Gamaliel's practice comprised a viable custom. In this approach, diaspora and Palestinian Jewry alike would have expressed high regard for Temple symbolism and institutions. But the trend to deprecate imitation, discernible in these mishnaic and toseftan sources, increased, so that in amoraic times, when the account of Todos was retold, the tradition was recast to represent sages (and not just unnamed individuals) responding not to Yose but directly to Todos, castigating him for misleading Roman Jewry and suggesting that he deserved to be put under a ban.[10]

If we consider the dynamic of the imitative act, we can probably understand why, in this case, it did not offer a lasting solution. In imitating, a person denies the existence of a change—in this case, the end of the sacrificial cult—and does not provide for a new means of observing the rite in question. The imitators must therefore be able to believe that the current practice is as meaningful and religiously effective as the old way. But regarding the passover offering, this surely would hold most strongly for those who valued the original sacrificial rite; it would not apply to the same degree, however, if at all, to those who had never gone on pilgrimage or who had never participated in the sacrifice. Moreover, could the old sacrificial rite, perceived as a celebration of national redemption, speak to a generation that knew no redemption and pinned its hopes on the future?

The approach of restructuring, on the other hand, responds to these ongoing needs and, in effect, turns the sacrifice into a non-essential part of the celebration by making the various non-sacrificial features independent of the cultic rite. Without rejecting the sacrifice, it assumes that the unleavened bread and bitter herbs are equal to it.

Rabbis faced two problems: first, to convince people that the rite without the sacrifice remained meaningful in traditional terms, and second, to respond to the new need posed by the loss of a national celebration in the capital. Hence, to insure that people would believe that the reconstructed arrangement embodied a proven ritual, rabbis created a precedent for the extra-sacrificial procedures in pre-70 practices outside the Temple. They claimed that the passover offering merely comprised a supplementary element added in the Temple precincts. With an anachronistic leap of faith, they depicted the new procedures as if they had always been the procedures. To solidify the belief in continuity with the past, they did not acknowledge that a change had taken place. Along with the restructuring, the early rabbis, moreover, introduced several elements that were not present or not important in the biblical rite but spoke to Jewry's new situation. The rabbis presented these as if they had formed part of the earlier rite. Once these additions were in place, the physical necessity of the sacrifice would appear less important.

Because we are interested in the transformation of the sacrifice, we now examine more closely how restructuring specifically affected the role of the offering. *M. Pesahim* 10:3 accomplishes the restructuring in a subtle fashion:

[A] [They] served him—he dips the lettuce [*hazeret*, that is, the vegetable used for the bitter herbs] before he reaches the bread condiment.

[B] [They] served him unleavened bread and lettuce and *haroset* [a mixture, e.g. of nuts, fruit and vinegar pounded together], even though the *haroset* is not a *mitzvah*. Rabbi Eleazar ben Zadok says, [It is a] *mitzvah*.

[C] And in the Temple [they] serve him the carcass of the passover offering.[11]

Equating the unleavened bread and bitter herbs with the passover sacrifice, the Mishnah declares that a person is served bitter herbs and unleavened bread and, it adds, in the Temple they add the sacrifice. Here is the key to the anachronistic, subtle presentation of the Mishnah—something often not appreciated because later printed editions of the Mishnah change the construction by making the reference into a past tense. The Mishnah then speaks not with a leap of anachronistic imagination but with a historical perspective. Instead of the Mishnah referring with a present participle to two contemporary practices (as we have printed it), the later revision of the Mishnah contrasts the present extra-Temple practice with a past Temple practice. To do this it adds the word *used to* to the sentence, "In the Temple precincts they [and this is the key addition] *used to* bring the body of the passover offering." But the Mishnah manuscripts and the parallel in the Tosefta enable us to restore the Mishnah's original reading and thus grasp the subtlety of its argument. As a result, a contemporary post-70 non-sacrificial rite gains a precedent in the pre-70 extra-Temple realm. That custom appears as the standard, while the Temple procedure is portrayed as involving the extra, sacrificial element.

M. Pesahim 10:4 applies the restructuring process to the Bible's pedagogic device of a parent instructing a child:

[A] [They] poured for him the second cup—
[B] and here the child asks, and if the child lacks intelligence, his father instructs him.
[C] How is this night different from all the [other] nights?
[D] For on all the [other] nights we eat leavened and unleavened bread; this night we eat only unleavened. For on all the [other] nights we eat meat roasted, steamed or cooked [= boiled]; this night only [or "all of it"] roasted.
[E] According to the child's intelligence, his father instructs him.
[F] [He] starts [reading] with the disgrace [section of the Bible] and ends with the glory;
[G] and [he] expounds [the biblical section] from "A wandering Aramean was my father" [Deut. 26:5] until he finishes the entire portion.[12]

Instead of the simple question of Exodus 12:25-27, which refers to putting blood on the doorposts and to making other preparations contingent on the sacrifice, the Mishnah suggests three questions which treat the *matzah*, *merorim*, and roasted meat, and in the process equates these three elements. The Mishnah specifically declares that at the pouring of the second cup the childs asks, and if he lacks intelligence, his father instructs him, why this night is different.

The parent is to respond not just by recounting the Israelite experience of transformation from slave to free person, but also by expounding the classic biblical text of Israel's history, which asserts that Israel *continues* to experience the divine bounty and redemption. Such an activity, called midrash, was especially emphasized by the rabbis, and provided for a broadening intellectual exercise that would enable people to find ever-new meaning in the celebration. The historical events and God's acts are what is essential, not the details of the paschal lamb.

M. Pesahim 10:5 enables us to see how the proposition that all is not lost without the sacrifice has been worked out:

[A] Rabban Gamaliel said, Whoever did not say these three things on Passover did not fulfill his obligation:
[B] *Pesah* [the passover offering], *matzah* [the unleavened bread], and *merorim* [the bitter herbs].
[C. 1] *Pesah*—because the Omnipresent skipped over [*pasah*] the houses of our ancestors in Egypt.
[C. 2] *Merorim*—because the Egyptians embittered [*meraru*] the lives of our ancestors in Egypt.
[C. 3] *Matzah*—because they were redeemed.
[D] Therefore we are obligated to give thanks, to praise, to glorify, to crown, to exalt, to elevate the One who did for us all these miracles and took us out of slavery to freedom, and let us say before Him Hallelujah [Psalm 113:1ff.].[13]

The Mishnah opens with a teaching of the first-century sage Rabban Gamaliel, declaring that people are to verbalize the three main objects: *pesah*, *matzah* and *merorim*. As we have seen in the previous *mishnayot*, the text makes the unleavened bread and bitter herbs as prominent as the sacrifice and decreases the sense of loss, since two of the three are still present in their original form. Further, by asserting that the mention of the three is what counts, the Mishnah takes the initial step away from the physical importance of the three elements, a trend expanded on by the authority who, in clause C, spells out the meaning of each of the three items. By supplying these rationales, the text gives significance to what the three foods represent rather than to the literal act of eating, and therefore provides a means of relating to them without their physical presence being consequential. It notably associates the fact of redemption with the unleavened bread and restricts the meaning of the sacrifice to the narrow act of protecting the homes of the Israelites in Egypt. As a result, the Mishnah alters significantly, though subtly, the perception of the paschal offering.

At this point we should take stock of the fact that the Mishnah, in the chapter as a whole and in this passage in particular, is constructing a reality through words. In encouraging us to understand the past and present through the sequence of words and acts it delineates, the text engineers our response to the notion of redemption. Note that it is the awareness of the meaning of *matzah* (C.3)—and not of the passover offering (C.1)—that produces the religious result of giving thanks to God, set out in clause D. This design accounts for the sequence of the three items in C varying, in the Mishnah manuscripts and early editions (and contrary to recent printed editions), from that of B, for if C were to follow B's sequence, the bitter experience under the Egyptians would inappropriately lead into D's requirement to thank God.[14]

According to D, one must give thanks to God by singing the appropriate biblical psalms and by reciting a blessing formula. This formula reminds people of past bounty so as to make them realize that they continue to experience it in the present. This is echoed in the phrase "who did for *us* all these miracles and took *us* out to freedom." The requirement in effect again restructures the biblical practice. Instead of Levites or other experts singing during the slaughtering of the paschal lamb, people without experts and even without the sacrifice are to offer thanksgiving. Since God continues to redeem Israel, Israel still experiences the divine presence. Hence, the past act—irrespective of the sacrifice—constitutes an act that redeems future generations as well, a thought pregnant for Jewry after the destruction of 70 C.E.

Other *mishnayot* set out the extent of the biblical psalms or Hallel, the use of blessings to highlight the message of redemption, the drinking of the third and fourth cups of wine, and the conclusion of the Hallel. The final mishnaic passage relevant to our theme (speaking anachronistically as if the sacrifice were still offered) avers that a person should not go on to after-dinner revelry after eating the paschal lamb, i.e., after the sacrificial meal. This rule, like a preceding mishnaic rule designed to avoid a drunken Hallel, aims at distinguishing the rite from a symposium or drinking party, which in antiquity was known as a frivolous meal centering on an ostensibly intellectual discussion. The need to take these steps became vital because the celebration lacked the passover sacrifice, which had supplied the earlier sacrificial meal version of the rite with a distinctive character. Now, as an intellectual ritual meal, it might be mistaken for—or degenerate into—a drinking banquet. But, like other ancient moralists, the rabbis wanted to preserve the religious character of the gathering. The rule, ostensibly relating to a situation when the offering was still brought, would apply as well even when it was not available.

We have discussed only part of the mishnaic reworking of the biblical heritage, which, in dislodging the meaning of the celebration from dependence on the offering, on the one hand, enabled a Festival of Passover to emerge separately from the sacrifice, and, on the other hand, demoted the sacrifice and removed it as the main factor or object both in the activity and in historical memory.

But while the Mishnah responds to the Temple's loss by restructuring the rite, it does not explicitly discuss the Temple's loss, and it contains just one passing allusion (in *M. Pesahim* 10:6) to the need to rebuild the Temple—and even this is presented as part of a statement of God's ongoing (or, following most readings: past) redemptive act. This lacuna points to an anomaly in the Mishnah; the earliest record of the seder reworks the biblical record, yet writes as if it presents nothing new. It is my contention that the mishnaic silence regarding the lost Temple is intentional, for if people openly acknowledged that loss, they would have to accept that the old structures are no longer viable. But the initial religious and psychological need of Jewry in the aftermath of the Temple's destruction was to believe that life could continue; for this reason, the early rabbis presented the new ways in old garb. The restructured rite would thereby be perceived as tried and true.[15] The Mishnah therefore focuses not on the trauma but on what was necessary in order to deal with that trauma, in effect working through the religious and psychological problem. The rabbis therefore employed a creative leap of imagination. As Alan Mintz aptly put it: "Alarmed at the effect the loss would have on the people, the rabbis *made believe* that there had been no rupture, and that the institutions they created or adapted had always existed."[16]

This transformation of the Passover rite from a pilgrimage experience leading up to a celebration of the national liberation into a home celebration, however, inevitably heightened the disparity between the ideal and the real, for in following a written script and a prescribed order, we are reminded of a reality that we do not experience in our everyday life. But as a ritual, setting aside the evening as a special event outside of normal time, the seder helps us overcome the contradictions of life. On the one hand, the anxiety and disappointment caused by unachievable ideals are temporarily eased by the experience of the ritual, where one feels intimate and integrated with one's fellow celebrants and in effect—at that moment—redeemed. Our disappointment and the dissonance we face are channelled into the rite itself. On the other hand, a person who receives a taste of the ideal may try to achieve it in daily life. We become invigorated to keep alive that ideal goal. But the cost of all this is to disregard the sacrifice—something with which the religious imagination would not be satisfied. The desire to re-incorporate the sacrifice takes us to the third chapter in our story.

III

Since post-mishnaic circles in Palestine (200-400) and Babylonia (200-600) no longer felt severe pain at the Temple's loss and began to treat the new ways as the established procedure, they were able openly to acknowledge that a change had taken place, in particular regarding the end of the sacrificial cult. They therefore extensively adapted the mishnaic order to the new reality.

These masters not only provided specific details and guidelines to effect the Mishnah's order, but also found significance and meaning in every detail of the rite. For them, the details did not comprise merely customary table manners, but rather participated in conveying the deeper significance of the event. Following the cue of the Mishnah, they pointed to reminders of redemption in various items other than the sacrifice. They taught that the drinking of the four cups symbolized redemption and divine retribution, and thereby admitted that Israel lacked redemption. They saw in the act of reclining not just a table manner expanded and applied even to the non-intellectual and the poor, but a symbolic act of freedom. They found in the *haroset*, a concoction commonly used as a dip for hors d'oeuvres, a meaning which heightened the sense of past slavery or of the divine providence that helped even in the midst of that slavery. They clearly highlighted the message that the past redemption applied to them and to every generation by expanding on the Mishnah's passing reference to this thought. For example, they provided separate texts stating that every generation should see itself as if it had been redeemed—a passage that has been interpolated into the printed editions of the Mishnah (*Pesahim* 10:5).

In this expansion, ritualizing and sacralizing of the seder,[17] they treated the paschal offering as a sacrifice without special symbolism of its own. The epitome of this transformation may be reflected in the amoraic supplementation of the Mishnah's special focus on the *matzah* and *merorim* (the bitter herbs), a requirement to lift up these two objects while speaking of them and a proscription on lifting the representation of the sacrifice. The rationale underscores how the passover sacrifice has become just another offering: it is to be avoided lest a person appear to be eating consecrated food outside the holy precincts.[18]

In a similar vein, Rav Huna states that the unleavened bread and bitter herbs (and *haroset*) are placed only before the person leading the recitation of the Haggadah (*Pesahim* 115b). The fact that the sacrifice has been replaced by the unleavened bread in particular may also be reflected in Samuel's tradition on the meaning of the unleavened bread. Perhaps expanding on a *baraita*, he sees the *matzah* not just as the bread of affliction but as the object over which the Haggadah is recited.[19] This adjustment likewise lies behind the later custom of finishing the meal with a taste of the unleavened bread, today called the *afikoman*, which is an adaptation of a mishnaic rule regarding closing the meal with the passover offering.[20]

The Amoraim supplement the Mishnah's list of items which are to be brought to the table with additional symbolic elements, most notably two cooked foods. These two cooked foods originally may have been designed to insure that the meal be a full festive meal, so to say, with two entrees; but soon they were seen as symbols of the lost passover and festival offerings. On our seder-plates, the shankbone serves as one of these symbolic objects. We can see the process at work in the following passage:

[A] For it is taught, Rabbi Yosi says, Even though he dipped the *hazeret*, it is a *mitzvah* to bring before him *matzah*,[21] *hazeret*, *haroset*, and two cooked foods....

[B] What are the "two cooked foods"?

[C] Said Rav Huna, Beets and rice....

[D] Hizkiah said, Even a fish with egg [cooked] on it.[22]
[E] Rav Yosef said, [A person] needs two types of meat, one in memory [*zekher*] of the paschal offering and one in memory of the festive offering.
[F] Ravina said, Even a bone with its broth.
(*Pesahim* 114b)

C-D assume that the foods are brought out of respect for the holiday in general. The author of these traditions apparently wanted to insure that those gathered even without the sacrifice partake of a complete holiday meal. E-F, on the other hand, sacralize the two foods, attributing to them special significance within the Passover context. They are to represent the lost sacrifices.

The process of symbolization serves a very important function for a community which recognizes that the current protocol differs from what traditionally had been perceived as the standard—a sacrificial meal centering on the paschal lamb—but which yet wants the current protocol to convey the same meaning as the lost order. People are able to retain the essence of the old protocol by preserving, despite the loss of the outer shell, the inner kernel of meaning by virtue of current words and actions that reveal that deeper meaning. To repeat, symbolic substitutes would not have proved popular at the initial step of overcoming the loss, because at that moment one does not want to confront the discontinuity. Indeed, just as it would be cruel to tell someone who suffered the loss of a spouse not to mourn that loss because the deceased's life is continued in his or her work and activities, so it would be cruel to the community to suggest that the lost shrine's meaning continues in what it symbolized and that the physical object could easily be replaced.

Accordingly, once people adapted to the loss of the cult, the lack of the sacrifice could be acknowledged. At that point, the hoped-for future redemption could be stressed, and symbolic acts and words could be introduced. The meaning of the old rite could continue without the sacrifice and the old structure. But this came about at the cost of lessened significance for the sacrifice itself. The foundation for this, to be sure, took place in *Pesahim* 10:5's expansion of Rabban Gamaliel's teaching, which shifts the notion of redemption from the sacrifice to the unleavened bread. A more restricted meaning for the offering, while true to the biblical record, is what remained.[23]

IV

A brief look at the medieval midrash *Exodus Rabbah* highlights the implications of the talmudic shift in the role of the sacrifice. This transformation led to the loss of the animal's original and inherent meaning, converting the representation of the paschal offering into a mere historical relic. In the following quotation, note how the midrash suggests that God prescribed the bringing of the passover offering only as a ruse so that Jews would circumcise themselves:

[A] "This is the ordinance [*hukat*] of the passover offering" [Exod. 12:43].

[B] Rabbi Simeon b. Halafta said, When Israel departed [or: were about to depart] from Egypt, the Holy One, Praised be He, said to Moses, Exhort the Israelites concerning the command of the passover offering. "No foreigner shall eat of it. But any slave a man has bought may eat of it once he has been circumcised" [Exod. 12:43b-44].

[C] When the Israelites saw that the uncircumcised were disqualified from eating the passover sacrifice, they arose with the least possible delay and circumcised all their servants and sons and all those who [subsequently] went out with them, as it says, "And the Israelites went and did so" [Exod. 12:28]. [This verse reports the Israelites' response to Moses's instructions to prepare the passover sacrifice. Cf. Exod. 12:50.]

[D] It can be compared to a king who arranged a banquet for his friends and who said, Unless the invited guests show my seal, none can enter. Similarly, God ordained a feast for them, "[flesh ...] roasted with fire, with unleavened bread and bitter herbs" [Exod. 12:8], because He delivered them from trouble; [but] He commanded, Unless the seal of Abraham is [inscribed] on your flesh, you cannot taste thereof.

[E] Thereupon all those who had been born in Egypt were immediately circumcised, and concerning these it is said, "Gather My devotees unto Me, those who made a covenant with Me for a sacrifice" [Ps. 50:5].

[F] And rabbis said, Israel did not wish to be circumcised in Egypt, and all save the tribe of Levi had abolished circumcision in Egypt, as it says, "And of Levi he said, Let Your Thummim and Urim be with Your faithful" [Deut. 33:8]. Why was this? "Your precepts alone they observed, and kept Your covenant" [Deut. 33:9]—in Egypt.

[G] And when the Holy One, Praised be He, was about to redeem them, He could find no merit in them. So what did he do? He called Moses and said, Go and circumcise them.

[H] (Some say Joshua was there and it was he who circumcised them, as it says, "And circumcise again the Israelites a second time" [Josh. 5:2].)

[I] But many of them would not agree to be circumcised. The Holy One, Praised be He, commanded that the passover offering should be prepared, and when Moses prepared the passover offering, God decreed that the four winds of the world [should blow] and they blew in the Garden of Eden.

[J] And from the winds that blew in the Garden of Eden [a scent] went and joined in that passover offering, for it says, "Awake, O north wind, Come, O south wind! Blow upon my garden, that its fragrance may spread" [Song 4:16]. And this scent spread over a distance of a forty days' journey.

[K] All the Israelites [then] came flocking to Moses and said, Do, please, give us some of your passover offering to eat, for they were famished on account of the odor that was in it.

[L] The Holy One, Praised be He, said, Unless you circumcise yourselves you cannot eat [thereof], as it says, "And the LORD said to Moses and Aaron: This is the ordinance of the passover offering," etc. [= "No foreigner shall eat of it. But any ... may eat of it once he has been circumcised" (Exod. 12:43)].

[M] Thereupon they immediately offered themselves for circumcision, and the blood of the passover offering mingled with that of circumcision.

[N] And the Holy One, Praised be He, took each one, kissed him and blessed him, as it says, "And when I passed by you and saw you wallowing in your blood," etc., [= "And I said to you, 'In thy blood live,' and I said to you, 'In thy blood live'" (Ezek. 16:6)]. "[In thy blood] live" refers to the blood of the passover offering; "[In thy blood] live" refers to the blood of circumcision.[24]

(*Exodus Rabbah*, "Bo" 19:5)

B-E and F-N both assume that the offering lacks any specific inherent meaning. The comments appropriately appear as interpretations of Exodus 12:43, which uses the word *hukah*, "ordinance" or "law," a term often understood as a divine command on ritual matters, especially for laws that appear to lack reasons. Both comments assume this perception of the passover sacrifice. According to the first interpretation, God prescribed the passover offering to induce the Israelites to circumcise themselves. The sacrificial meal must then take on new meaning, and it appears as a banquet to commemorate the deliverance, as if the liberation had already taken place. The second interpretation is even more explicit in playing down the sacrifice. Reworking a tradition found in *Mekhilta* "Pisha" 5, clauses G and N make the circumcision the sole focus of interest, with the sacrifice left obliterated.[25]

V

Tracing the history of the sacrifice has thus provided us with a window through which to see the development of the seder as a whole. The seder originally emerged in response to a particular crisis, centering on the loss of the passover sacrifice, and it reflects the religious issues of that day. Although some tried imitative acts to perpetuate the passover sacrificial rite, the approach that was to become dominant in rabbinic Judaism eschewed exact imitations of the past—for by eating an animal prepared in imitation of the sacrifice one would remain totally tied to the past and unable to direct one's energies to meeting current reality, whether to overcome it or to adapt things to it. Yet in confronting this reality, since the rabbis initially could not totally embrace the new situation, at least in appearance they chose continuity; they needed reassurance that the connection with God the redeemer, who took "us" out of Egypt, would remain effective and meaningful. Hence they restructured the rite, enabling people to act, say and believe that what was done today, while not replicating the Temple cult, existed as well in Temple days but was not contingent on the sacrifice. The restructuring itself, however, would undergo an expansion process and symbolization which found new meaning in the seder's words and actions. As I have argued elsewhere, the religious mind, especially in dealing with rituals, constantly searches to discover meaning and to articulate and reformulate ideas so as to keep them vibrant. Once the function of the passover sacrifice and the notions associated with it had been taken over by the unleavened bread, it was but a small step to forgetting or disregarding the original *raison d'etre* of the sacrifice. We may therefore understand why even the symbolic substitute for the offering has become a historical relic which serves only to remind people of what took place. The symbols that elicit a resonance in people and that continue to nurture them are those that remain viable in themselves and not as mere replacements. To understand how that process expanded and transformed the role and meaning of the unleavened bread is another story, for another occasion.[26]

1. For full discussion, documentation, and bibliography on the development of the seder, including references to the important works by Meir Friedmann, Daniel E. Goldschmidt and Joseph Tabory, see Baruch M. Bokser, *The Origins of the Seder* (Berkeley, 1984), to which add idem, "Was the Last Supper a Passover Seder?" *Bible Review* 3 (Summer 1987): 24-33; idem, "Todos and Rabbinic Authority in Rome," in *Religion, Literature and Society in Ancient Israel: Formative Judaism,* New Perspectives on Ancient Judaism, Vol. 1, ed. Jacob Neusner et al. (Lanham, Md., 1987); and idem, "Ritualizing the Seder," *Journal of the American Academy of Religion* 56 (Fall 1988): 443-473.

2. Comparable questions appear in Exodus 13:8, responding to the commandment to eat unleavened bread seven days, and Exodus 13:14-16, dealing with the dedication or redemption of firstborn humans and animals to mark the slaying of the firstborn Egyptians as part of the tenth plague. A fourth instance, from Deut. 6:20, treats the commandments in general and not Passover in particular.

3. Cf., however, Nahum Sarna, *Exploring Exodus* (New York, 1986), 92-93.

4. See, e.g., Josephus, *Wars* 6:423-24, trans. H. St. J. Thackeray et al., Loeb Classical Library, 9 vols. (Cambridge, 1926-65), 3:498-99; and Bokser, *Origins,* 24-25 and nn.

5. Philo, *Special Laws,* 2:145-46, trans. F. H. Colson et al., Loeb Classical Library, 12 vols. (Cambridge, 1929-62), 7:394-97.

6. This may even be attested in the Elephantine sources; see Bokser, *Origins,* 20-21.

7. Additionally, if there is credibility in the belief of certain first- or second-century rabbis, some diaspora Jews might have broiled meat in imitation of the passover lamb, though it is unclear whether such reports refer to a pre- or post-70 period. See Bokser, *Origins,* 101-6; and below.

8. Victor Turner, "Pilgrimage as Social Process," in idem, *Dramas, Fields, and Metaphors* (Ithaca, 1974), 166-230.

9. See, e.g., *M. Zevahim* 2:2, 5; ch. 5, esp. 5:8 (and Albeck, *Shisha Sidrei Mishnah,* 6 vols. [Jerusalem, 1954-59], 5:356); *T. Zevahim* 2:1 (p. 481, ll. 14-24); and *M. Hullin* 6:2.

10. See *Y. Pesahim* 7:1 (34a), *Beitzah* 2:7 (61c), and *Mo'ed Katan* 3:1 (81d); and *B. Beitzah* 23a, *Pesahim* 53a-b, and *Berakhot* 19a; and Bokser, "Todos," which analyzes the history of these traditions and suggests why post-mishnaic circles were led to revise the earlier account. On other rabbinic sources and non-rabbinic references adduced to support the argument that some Jews continued to eat a substitute or an actual passover offering, see Bokser, *Origins,* 101-6.

11. We follow the Kaufmann and other MSS and early printed editions. See Saul Lieberman, *Tosefta ki-Feshutah,* 8 vols. (New York, 1955-), 4:654; Bokser, *Origins,* 119, nn. 6-9; and below.

12. On the text, selection and sequence of the questions, we follow the Kaufmann and other manuscript readings which are further attested in such works as Alfasi; see Bokser, *Origins,* 119, nn. 10-12.

13. We follow the Kaufmann and other MSS and early editions regarding the text and sequence of the passage; see Bokser, *Origins,* 119-20, n. 13.

14. This has been obscured in later Mishnah editions and in the Haggadah, which interpolate a paragraph between C and D that speaks of every generation feeling redeemed. This addition enables C to close with the mention of the bitter herbs without bitterness appearing as the basis for thanksgiving. The rise in the *matzah*'s importance

and the intrusion of the Festival of Unleavened Bread and its themes into the seder is further extended in most (excepting several early) Haggadot, which replace the rationale for the *matzah* with a quote from Exod. 12:39 that speaks of the haste in leaving Egypt preventing the unleavened bread from rising. See Joseph Tabory, "Towards a Characterization of the Passover Meal" (in Hebrew), *Bar-Ilan Annual* 18-19 (1981): 72-74, esp. n. 23.

15. This is in accord with the Mishnah's overall outlook, as suggested by Jacob Neusner, *Judaism: The Evidence of the Mishnah* (Chicago, 1981), and its portrayal of the cultic Temple realm not in archaeological depictions but rather in narrative accounts with their own agendum, as recognized by Benzion Wacholder, *Messianism and Mishnah*, The Louis Caplan Lecture on Jewish Law, March 29, 1978 (Cincinnati, 1979), and Yonah Frankel, *Iyyunim be-Olamo ha-Ruhani shel Sippur ha-Aggadah* (Tel Aviv, 1981), 119-121.

16. Alan Mintz, review of Bokser, *Origins*, in *The New Republic*, 22 April 1985, 42 (emphasis in the original). On the anachronism, cf. Tabory, "Characterization," 70.

17. See Bokser, "Ritualizing."

18. *B. Pesahim* 116b, on which cf. 1 Cor. 11:24. The printed editions add a second element to the reason, "lest one also appear to set aside an animal as holy," which may be a gloss generated from *B. Pesahim* 53a-b. See the readings in the early commentaries, and Raphaelo Rabbinovicz, *Dikdukei Soferim: Tractate Pesahim* (Munich, 1874; reprint, New York, 1960), 364, to which add Columbia MS; and cf. David Halivni, *Sources and Traditions* (in Hebrew), 4 vols. (Tel Aviv and Jerusalem, 1968-82), tractates *Erubin* and *Pesahim*, 426-29.

19. *B. Pesahim* 115b-116, which explains Deut. 16:3's name for unleavened bread, *lehem oni*, in two fashions. In addition to the views metaphorically connecting the meaning to the method of the *matzah*'s preparation (a rationale also found in *Mekhilta* "Pisha" 10 [Horowitz-Rabin ed. p. 35]), another view sees it as the object over which the Haggadah is recited (*onin alav*). Judith Hauptmann, *The Evolution of the Talmudic Sugya: A Comprehensive Source Critical Analysis of Sugyot Containing Braitot Introduced by* Tanya Nami Hakhi (Ph.D. diss., Jewish Theological Seminary of America, New York, 1982), 312-315, argues that the latter position was first articulated by Samuel (whose comment entered the baraita). If correct, a third-century amora would be adding an insight by drawing on the ritual use of the *matzah*.

20. See *B. Pesahim* 119b-120a; especially Menahem Ha-Meiri, *Beit ha-Behirah* (Jerusalem, 1967); and Joseph Tabory, "The Passover Eve Ceremony—An Historical Outline," *Imanuel* 12 (1981): 35, n. 9.

21. In Columbia and other MSS; Rabbinovicz, 356, n. 40.

22. Columbia MS and several other readings lack the word "on it" (Rabbinovicz, 356, n. 90) which, given the parallels cited below, does not change the meaning.

23. Note as well *M. Pesahim* 10:9, in which Akiba subtly downgrades the special role and significance of the paschal lamb, in effect treating it as any other sacrifice, on which see Bokser, *Origins*, 48. It is also reflected in the action of those who glossed the Mishnah with words acknowledging the distance from the sacrifice, adding the "used to" to 10:3's reference to the Temple practice and interpolating the mention of the "two cooked foods" into 10:4; see Bokser, *Origins*, 95-96.

24. On the text and interpretation of this passage, see Bokser, *Origins*, 96-99 and nn.

25. The reuse of the *Mekhilta* tradition helps explain M-N's mention of the blood of the passover offering.

26. Cf. Ruth Freedman, *The Passover Seder* (Philadelphia, 1981); and Tabory, "Characterization."

Islam and the Jews: Myth, Counter-Myth, History[*]
by
Mark R. Cohen

You know, my brethren, that on account of our sins God has cast us into the midst of this people, the nation of Ishmael, who persecutes us severely, and who devises ways to harm us and to debase us.... No nation has ever done more harm to Israel. None has been able to reduce us as they have.

Thus wrote Maimonides to the persecuted Jews of Yemen late in the twelfth century. In recent years the issue addressed by him has aroused new and impassioned interest—indeed, a highly politicized debate, in books, articles, and public forums—on the question: How did the Jews fare under Islamic rule in the Middle Ages? Were they treated better than their brethren in Europe, or was their situation perhaps similar to, if not, as Maimonides suggests, worse than, that of the persecuted Jews of Christendom?

Two radically divergent answers to this question have been offered. One is the well-known thesis—or rather, *myth*—of the Jewish-Islamic interfaith utopia, a "golden age" of toleration, of political achievement, and of remarkably integrated cultural efflorescence. This myth was invented by nineteenth-century European Jewish intellectuals frustrated by the tortuously slow progress of their own integration into Gentile society in the age of emancipation; it went hand-in-hand with the so-called "lachrymose conception" of European Jewish history, according to which Jewish life in medieval Christian Europe was one long chain of suffering.

Originally promulgated by Jewish writers, the myth of Judeo-Islamic harmony (contrasted with Judeo-Christian conflict) has in our own time been appropriated by Arabs and by Western sympathizers with the Arab struggle against Israel, who attempt, through the use of history, to explain and in fact justify modern Arab anti-Zionism and anti-Semitism. They argue, explicitly or implicitly, that the current disharmony between Jews and Arabs is not to be attributed to any long-standing Arab or Islamic anti-Semitism. Rather, as Jewish historians have claimed, Jews and Arabs lived in peace and friendship for centuries; therefore, the source of modern Arab antipathy towards Israel is the Jews themselves, who destroyed the old harmony when they began to threaten Muslim-Arab rights to the land of Palestine.

An early example of this adoption of the Jewish myth of the interfaith utopia can be found in George Antonius' book, *The Arab Awakening*.[1] Among more recent publications are Ibrahim Amin Ghali's *Le monde arabe et les juifs*,[2] and, in Arabic, Qasim 'Abduh Qasim's *Al-yahud fi Misr mundh al-fath al-islami hatta al-ghazw al-'uthmani* (The Jews of Egypt from the Islamic Conquest to the Ottoman Invasion),[3] as well as the paper given by Said Abdel Fattah Ashour at the Fourth Conference of the Academy of Islamic Research at Al-Azhar University in Cairo in September, 1968. (Entitled *"Al-yahud fi 'l-'usur al-wusta: dirasa muqarina bayn al-sharq wa-'l-gharb,"* it was published both in the Arabic original[4] and in the official English translation of the conference proceedings[5] under the title, "Jews in the Middle Ages: Comparative Study of East and West.")

Dismayed by contemporary Arab exploitation of the myth of the interfaith utopia in the service of the cause against Israel, some Jewish writers have, lamentably, invented a "counter-myth" to take its place. Echoing and often citing Maimonides' dark view of Islamic treatment of the Jews, these writers indict Islam as congenitally and relentlessly persecutory. And, by transposing the theory of Jewish suffering from Christendom to Islam, they have created what may be called the "neo-lachrymose" conception of the Jewish past.[6]

One well-known promulgator of this revisionist trend suffered personal humiliation when she was expelled along with other Jews from Egypt in 1956. Writing under the pseudonym *Bat Ye'or*, "Daughter of the Nile," she has published several pamphlets and books sounding the theme of congenital and unremitting Arab-Islamic persecution of the non-Muslim religions. Her French book on the subject has appeared in an expanded English version called *The Dhimmi: Jews and Christians Under Islam*[7], and it constitutes a classic example of this revisionist trend. Another is journalist Joan Peters' *From Time Immemorial: The Origins of the Arab-Jewish Conflict over Palestine*.[8] This work has gained considerable notoriety for its provocative assault upon the historical argument defending Arab claims to the land of Palestine. In her introductory chapters Peters presents a litany of instances of anti-Jewish persecution in the pre-modern Islamic world, arguing overtly against Arab rhetoric espousing the myth of the interfaith utopia as well as against the view, shared by many Jewish and non-Jewish writers alike, "that the Jews were, during certain periods in the Arab lands, 'better off' than they were in Christian lands of Europe."

While the myth of the interfaith utopia was certainly in need of correction, the counter-myth, with its implicit transvaluation of the older conception of the relative status of the Jews of the West and the East, does not represent a fairer reading of the past. A more balanced approach, such as that taken by Bernard Lewis in his book, *The Jews of Islam*,[9] or by Norman Stillman in the historical introduction to his source book, *The Jews of Arab Lands*,[10] is badly needed. That is because, as any careful and systematic reading of the historical evidence shows, despite the theological intolerance that Islam shared with Christendom, the Jews of Islam experienced far greater security and far more integration with the majority society than their brethren in Europe. During the first six centuries of Islam, the period embracing the so-called "Golden Age" that has been the focus of attention by proponents of both the old myth and the new counter-myth, the incidence of violent persecution, with great loss of life, was comparatively low. The discriminatory restrictions of the so-called Pact of 'Umar, most of them adopted from Byzantine-Christian anti-Jewish legislation, were more often than not observed in the breach. Such irrational conceptions as the association of the Jews with the Devil, a well-known feature of the medieval Christian attitude towards the Jew, had little place even in the popular Arab imagination. Blood libels—in Europe a by-product of the popular perception of the diabolical Jew—were absent during these centuries. Expulsions did not occur. And we hear practically nothing during this period about prosecution of Jewish converts to Islam for alleged unfaithfulness to the new religion.

If theology did not dispose Muslims to treat Jews better than they were treated in Christendom, what accounts for the relatively more favorable position of the Jews of the medieval Islamic world? The answer, as might be expected, is complex and nuanced, involving economic, political and social factors that interacted in history in ways that elude simple description. Moreover, the contrast is starker for Northern than for Southern Europe, where the persistence of pre-Christian Roman traditions and the older settlement of Jews, bordering on indigenous habitation, seem to have fostered a more tolerant and economically and socially more integrated environment. What we shall have to say, therefore, in what follows takes *Northern* Christendom as its point of comparison so that the contrast will be sharpened with more meaningful distinctions brought to bear on the discussion.

As is well known, Jews came to Europe during the early Middle Ages principally as international merchants. Christian rulers, particularly the Carolingian kings, encouraged Jewish traders to settle in their realms by offering them favorable conditions of residency and commercial mobility. The Jews, indeed, fulfilled an important function in this predominantly rural and agricultural setting. However, their economic role was simultaneously a cause of social resentment. As merchants, Jews found themselves practitioners of a marginal and despised profession. Continuing a prejudice characteristic of Roman society, early medieval Christendom held the trader in relatively low repute. Always on the move and lacking firm roots in any given locale, the merchant appeared quintessentially alien. This attitude was reinforced by Christian doctrines about the "just price" that placed commerce at the bottom end of the scale of religiously acceptable walks of life. From the outset, therefore, the identification—however exaggerated—of Jews with a despised occupation accentuated their own alien religious status within Christian society.

This situation degenerated when, with the revival of urban life in eleventh-century Europe, Christians began to enter commerce on a large scale. Formerly the despised, alien merchant in a backward rural environment, the Jewish merchant now became a resented commercial competitor. As commercial guilds developed, Jews were excluded from membership on account of their inability to take the required Christian oath of initiation. The result, well known to all, is that Jews who were involved in commerce gradually transferred their energies to usury. And other Jews who for various reasons were pressured out of productive occupations also found their only means of livelihood in making loans to Christians. Jewish banking complemented European economic expansion during the high Middle Ages, and, because Jewish profits from moneylending steadily filled and refilled royal treasuries in the form of tax revenues, secular rulers sanctioned and gave legal support to this enterprise.

If kings and emperors tolerated the Jews on account of their economic benefit to the royal treasury, in Christian society at large moneylending bred anti-Jewish contempt. Jewish usurers were universally hated. Hatred emanated both from the common folk, who were the Jews' main pawnbroking customers, and from elements of the new Christian bourgeoisie, who resented the royal support for Jewish usury. Dependence upon the Jewish moneylender created an improper inversion of the well-defined hierarchical relationship between Christianity and Judaism and intensified the degree of discomfort with the alien Jewish presence. These anti-Jewish sentiments were further reinforced by the Catholic church's vigorous campaign against the evil of usury beginning in the twelfth century. Although only sporadically successful in gaining the support of secular rulers, it had a devastating effect on Jewish economic well-being wherever it fell upon receptive ears. In short, economic factors, intertwined with religious conceptions, played an ongoing role in molding the negative attitude towards the Jews in Europe of the Middle Ages and in creating the rigid boundaries that separated Jews and Christians from one another.

In Islam, by contrast, religious conceptions and economic realities combined to produce a different state of affairs. Unlike Christianity, Islam, influenced by the mercantile background of Muhammad's native city Mecca, was born with a positive attitude towards commerce. The example of Muhammad's own life, as well as statements in the Qur'an and in other Islamic holy literature, lent strong support to the mercantile life. And, since many of the jurists in the early Islamic period were themselves merchants, Islamic law was shaped to meet the needs of a mercantile economy. On purely religious grounds, therefore, there was no basis in Islam for the kind of prejudicial attitude towards the Jewish merchant that existed from the outset in Christendom.

In addition to this fundamental distinction in economic "theory," economic realities during the early Islamic centuries prevented the development of the competitive atmosphere that heightened anti-Jewish sentiment in the West during the period of urban-commercial expansion. The Islamic conquest, with its political unification of the entire Mediterranean and all of southwest Asia, set in motion an enormous commercial revolution and created unlimited economic opportunities. As a result, whereas in Europe the new Christian merchants of the high Middle Ages viewed the old Jewish merchants as competitors to be displaced, in Islam Muslim merchants of the early centuries following the conquest saw the Jews as equal participants in a burgeoning imperial economy. Interdenominational cooperation was common, and commercial guilds excluding all but co-confessors of the dominant faith did not yet exist. Moreover, the Jews enjoyed extensive economic diversification. This made the Jews more "like" their non-Jewish neighbors and reduced the level of hostility, which in Europe resulted in part from their economic marginality. Of equal importance, the Jews of Islam during this period (and later on, for that matter) were never restricted to moneylending, as were their coreligionists in Northern Europe by about the twelfth century. Jews and Muslims borrowed and lent from and to one another, and the sticky issue of usurious lending to Gentiles that caused so much consternation and insecurity for Jews in medieval Europe, leading rabbis to inveigh against the practice, had virtually no counterpart either within or without the Jewish community of medieval Islam.

While economically the Jews of Islam experienced much more freedom and integration into Gentile society than their brethren in Europe, legally their situation appears comparable, if not worse. Proponents of the counter-myth regularly point to the humiliating disabilities imposed upon the Jews (and Christians) in the Pact of 'Umar and kindred Islamic sources. These stipulations include prohibitions against building or repairing houses of worship, against holding public religious ceremonies, against bearing arms or riding anything but the least honorable mounts, against holding public office, as well as a poll tax (*jizya*) levied in humiliating fashion. It is often noted, too, that the infamous "Jewish badge" introduced in Europe for the first time in the thirteenth century existed centuries earlier in the Pact of 'Umar's stipulations requiring distinctive dress. The twin themes of segregation and humiliation that run through the Islamic sources seem to rival if not exceed the legal restrictions and pariah status imposed upon the Jews in the Christian West.

Historically, however, theory and practice diverged. Even some proponents of the counter-myth concede that by and large the restrictions of the Pact of 'Umar were very unevenly and sporadically enforced during the centuries under discussion here. The large number of synagogues that were built to accommodate the new Jewish communities of the expanding Islamic world, and the frequent reference in our sources to the reimposition of the Pact of 'Umar restrictions, testify to the relative ease with which Jews and Christians evaded the heavy hand of the law.

Moreover, in assessing the legal position of the Jews of Islam it is important to reassert that the basic terminology defining their legal status, the *dhimma*, conveys the idea of "protection," which the Pact of 'Umar explicitly guarantees the Jews and Christians (*dhimmis*) in return for their recognition of the superiority of Islam. The book by Bat Ye'or mentioned above, which espouses the counter-myth of "thirteen centuries of sufferings and humiliations" under Islam, creates a grossly misleading impression by characterizing every bleak aspect of the Judeo-Islamic experience as "the *dhimmi* condition."

Equally important, any comparative analysis of the position of the Jews under medieval Islam and Christianity must take into account a fundamental political difference between the two societies. Medieval Christendom had two competing authority structures, the state and the church, which were plagued by endless conflict. Popes and secular rulers battled with words and sometimes with armies for supreme authority over the Christian masses, and each side vied for hegemony over the Jews as well. Kings and emperors claimed the prerogative to protect the Jews, whom some began to call "serfs of the royal chamber." Relegated to a special legal status, Jews became subject to all the advantages and disadvantages of unmediated dependence upon the secular ruler. When central authority was strong, Jews could generally count on royal or baronial protection. But this protection was accompanied by rapacious taxation that sorely threatened Jewish financial security. When central power was weak, or when the ruler was far away, popular hostility towards the Jews often spilled over, unchecked, into physical violence.

The Roman church, for its part, strove to achieve the universalist ideal of a Christendom ruled by direct apostolic successors to Peter. Beginning in the thirteenth century, it asserted the theological doctrine of the "perpetual servitude" of the Jews. The church insisted that secular rulers eliminate state-supported Jewish usury and segregate Jews from their Christian neighbors. The tribulations which afflicted the Jews as a result of the church's partial, and in the case of Jewish moneylending occasionally greater than expected, success in enforcing its will in these matters—like the very fact of the Jews' tenuous direct dependence upon the protection of the kings and emperors of Europe—may be credited to their unenviable position as pawns in the battle between church and state in the Middle Ages.

The somewhat less precarious position of the Jews in the medieval Islamic world has much to do with the fundamentally different organization of political authority in Islam. Unlike Christendom, classical Islam, being an ecclesiastical polity, knows no formal division between church and state. The caliph embodies secular and religious leadership in one and the same person. Consequently, medieval Islam did not experience a church-state struggle, nor its untoward side effects on the Jewish minority. To be sure, Islamic rulers were not immune to the conservative sentiments of clerics who favored strict enforcement of the Pact of 'Umar and even the revocation of its protective guarantees when *dhimmis* violated its ordinances. Many instances of anti-Jewish and anti-Christian oppression can be traced directly to the intolerant voices of these *'ulama*. Nonetheless, this was relatively rare during the first six centuries of Islam, when religious scholars had somewhat less influence in public affairs than they did later on. Moreover, as A. L. Udovitch has pointed out in an important essay,[11] in Islamic law the status of the Jews is nowhere treated as a separate issue. Rather, stipulations are incorporated subject by subject into the conventional categories of the classical Islamic law codes. This stands in sharp contrast to the isolation of Jewry law provisions in the law of medieval Christian states and is a reflection of the greater degree of integration of the Jew in medieval Muslim society. Also, by way of contrast, the Jews of Islam never became direct, legal dependents of the ruler; nor did the Pact of 'Umar link toleration of Jews to their economic utility, as was the case in Europe. These differences surely help explain why the expulsions of the Jews in the West were not duplicated in the medieval Islamic world.

Not only were there differences in the legal policies of Christendom and Islam towards the Jews. The Jews held a disparate status within the social structure of the two societies as well. As noted above, the mercantile activities of the Jews accentuated their image in Christian Europe as a marginal group. Nonetheless, they experienced a considerable degree of security and prosperity, especially in the Carolingian kingdom. This was largely a consequence of the pluralistic structure of early medieval European civilization, which was still imperfectly Christianized and in which the Barbarian legal principle of the personality of law was still strong. In this heterogeneous environment, the Jews could be tolerated despite their own religious non-conformity and cultural and legal distinctiveness. By the eleventh century, however, the last remaining pagans of Western Europe had been converted to Christianity, leaving the Jews as the only non-Christian entity in society. The concomitant spread of the notion of a universalistic Catholicism, mediated to the masses by the monastic orders, also dealt a blow to the tolerance that was associated with the earlier, more pluralistic age. By the eleventh century, these and other transformations in Western Christendom, including the growing economic competition, set the stage for the anti-Jewish violence of the age of the Crusades.

The position of the Jew in medieval Near Eastern society stands in sharp contrast. The Jews were, first of all, indigenous inhabitants of the area, not, as in Western Christendom, immigrant aliens. In addition, pluralism and religious heterogeneity were more deeply and more permanently ingrained in Islamic than in European Christian society. A multiplicity of ethnic Muslim groups—Arabs, Turks, Berbers, and Iranians—populated the social landscape along with the Jews. As religious dissenters, moreover, Jews were not unique. They shared their *dhimmi* status with other non-Muslim groups, principally the Christians and the Zoroastrians. As a result, Muslim religious discrimination was directed at the *dhimmi* class as a whole, rather than at the Jews in particular. And while it is true that the Qur'an and later Arabic literature occasionally distinguish between the two subordinate monotheistic religions, evincing a certain slight preference for the Christians, it is also accurate to say that contempt for nonbelievers in Islam was usually more or less evenly distributed across the *dhimmi* class. Moreover, when the restrictive clauses of the Pact of 'Umar were, on occasion, rigorously enforced, they were usually directed in the first instance at the far more numerous Christians. For all these reasons, therefore, the negative psychological impact of second-class status was substantially blunted for the Jews. To be sure, as in Christian Europe, the Jews were always and everywhere viewed by Muslims as social and religious inferiors. In practice, however, the Jews of Islam were less rigidly set off from the majority society than were the Jews of Christendom.

The permeability of boundaries between Jews and Muslims was fostered by yet another distinguishing characteristic of Islamic society—it was far less corporate than its European counterpart. In Islam there did not exist to the same extent the more or less rigidly defined identity (reinforced by royal concessions of legal autonomy) that Western corporate organization formally assigned to such groups as the nobility, merchant guilds, the clergy, municipalities, and, of course, the Jews. Rather, social agglutinates relied on informal ties of loyalty and group identity that by their very nature allowed for flexibility and an overlapping of roles and tended to mitigate the marginality to which official Islamic theology assigned the Jews. Though deprived of the right to bear arms and hence excluded from one of the most powerful groups in Muslim society, namely, the army, Jews participated in most of its other major social categories: the merchant class, the crafts, the government bureaucracy, and even the agricultural sector. Moreover, the absence of rigid corporate social organization in Islam meant that collective guilt for alleged crimes against the host society and its religion, so commonly assigned in Christendom to the Jewish corporate entity, did not become an operative motif in the Islamic-Jewish relationship. These realities were reinforced by the persistence in Islam of the principle of the personality of law long after it was replaced in Christendom by territorial and municipal legal codes that relegated the Jews to the position of a grudgingly tolerated, separate and alien non-Christian corporate group.

Economic, political, and social factors acted in Islam as a counterweight to the fundamental theological hostility towards the religion of Judaism (branded as an inferior version of monotheism) and towards the Jews (stigmatized, along with the Christians, as contemptible infidels). However, even the theological position of Islam vis-à-vis the Jews differed significantly from that of Christianity. In Christendom, theological opposition to Judaism and the Jews was firmly rooted in the historical situation attending the rise of the new religion; it formed an organic and essential ingredient in Christian thought. Born directly out of Judaism, promulgated originally by professing Jews, and lacking an independent ethnic base, Christianity, from its inception, found itself locked in a bitter struggle to incorporate and then differentiate itself from its Jewish parent. Desperately needing to win converts from among the "Gentiles" in order to insure its existence, the early Church bitterly resented Jewish proselytizing among the Roman pagans, not to speak of Jewish resistance to the Christian mission. Moreover, until the fourth century the Roman government suspected the Christian community of messianic subversion and relentlessly persecuted the neophytes while continuing its ancient policy of recognizing the legitimacy of Judaism and protecting the Jews. In an effort to win its own recognition from pagan Rome and to justify its own sense of superiority, the nascent Church developed an elaborate anti-Jewish theological doctrine. This doctrine stated that since the Jews had rejected Christ, God had rejected the Jews and had chosen the Christians in their stead as the new Israel.

When Christianity became the official religion of the Roman Empire, following the conversion of Emperor Constantine at the beginning of the fourth century, the theology of divine rejection was systematically employed to whittle away at the protective provisions of Roman Jewry law. At the same time, the spiritual Fathers of the Church, led by St. Augustine, developed a theological rationale for the continued presence of the Jews in Christian society. This was the well-known doctrine of "witness," according to which God had preserved the Jews as living testimony, by virtue of their abject state, to the victory of Christianity. And, with their conversion to Christianity at the time of the Second Coming, they would bear witness to the truth of Jesus' Messianic essence. This official church doctrine provided a rationale for protecting the Jews and served to temper the theological animosity that informed the earliest phase of the Judeo-Christian relationship.

In the Middle Ages, the heightened piety of the age of the Crusades brought a new, popular brand of Christian anti-Jewishness to the fore. Its most ominous manifestation was the wholesale massacre of the Jews of the Rhineland in the Crusader pogroms of 1096. Popular mentality, partly to justify the violence, and fed by uneducated local clergy, embellished the official Catholic theology of rejection by fixating on the Jew as the ally of the devil, bent on destroying Christendom. The vulgar anti-Jewish theology of the high and later Middle Ages, with its frequent blood libels and pogroms, was paralleled by a somewhat more civilized, though no less threatening, assault on the religion of Judaism, manifested in disputations designed to persuade Jews to convert to Christianity.

From statements in the Qur'an, the prophetic traditions (the *hadith*), and other portions of its religious and secular literature, Islam appears similar to Christianity in its theological opposition to the Jews and Judaism. Moreover, while in Christendom massacres of the Jews began relatively late in the history of the relationship of the two faiths, in Islam the very first encounter between Islam and Judaism produced a violent anti-Jewish pogrom. The Prophet Muhammad, having experienced ridicule and opposition from the Jews of

Medina, lashed out violently by expelling some and massacring an entire Jewish tribe. However, that brutal anti-Jewish episode in the early Judeo-Islamic relationship turned out to have been—relatively speaking—an isolated one. This can be explained comparatively by the particular historical circumstances in which Islam originated and spread.

Unlike Christianity, Islam did not need to establish its identity at the expense of its Jewish parent. Islam was established on a solid ethnic foundation, the tribes of the Arabian Peninsula, who were swiftly won over to the new religion. Conquering within decades the rest of the Near Eastern and the North African world, Islam achieved virtually overnight what it had taken Christianity nearly three centuries to accomplish. There was even less reason, therefore, to continue the aggressive struggle against Judaism, let alone devise a theology of divine rejection.

In addition, because Muhammad was not a Messiah, Islam, unlike Christianity, never conceived of itself as being a messianic fulfillment of Judaism. Rather, Islam saw itself as a restoration and purification of Abrahamic monotheism, which had become eroded in earlier divinely inspired religions, in Christianity more than in Judaism. The Jewish rejection of Muhammad, therefore, never entailed the same theological challenge to Islam that was implicit in the Jewish rejection of Jesus. Hence, Islam did not invest anywhere near the same polemical energies expended by Christendom to refute Judaism and to convert the Jews.

Characteristically, the Muslim attitude towards Jewish Scripture differed from that of its Christian counterpart. Christianity needed the Jewish Bible—the Old Testament, in its parlance—as witness to the incarnation and mission of Christ described in the New Testament. Islam viewed its Scripture differently, as a replacement of the divinely revealed, yet humanly distorted, Scriptures of both Judaism and Christianity. Muhammad, having personally rediscovered pure, Abrahamic monotheism through a new divine revelation, did not need the Jewish Bible for the justification of Islam. And indeed, the various attempts by medieval Muslim writers to find annunciations of the mission of Muhammad in biblical verses pale in significance when compared to the massive Christological exegesis of Jewish Scripture. Rabbinic exegesis of the Bible—so repugnant to Christian theologians—bothered Muslim clerics only insofar as it distorted pristine Abrahamic monotheism. Thus the Islamic polemic against the rabbis was much less virulent and had far less serious repercussions. The Talmud was burned in Paris, not in Cairo or Baghdad.

More secure than their brethren in the Christian West, the Jews of Islam took a correspondingly more conciliatory view of their rulers. In Europe, the Jews nurtured a pronounced hatred for Christians, whom they considered to be idolators subject to the anti-pagan discriminatory provisions of the ancient Mishnah. Moreover, when faced with the choice between death and conversion, the Jews of Northern Europe usually chose martyrdom rather than "the polluting waters of the baptismal font," as they called it in Hebrew. The Jews of Islam had a markedly different attitude towards the religion of their masters. Staunch Muslim opposition to polytheism convinced Jewish thinkers like Maimonides of Islam's unimpeachable monotheism. This essentially "tolerant" Jewish view of Islam echoed Islam's own respect for the Jewish "people of the Book" and doubtless constituted a factor—alongside the extensive contact in the economic and social spheres that tended to blur the boundaries between Jew and Muslim—disposing Jews faced with persecution at the hands of Islam to convert rather than suffer martyrdom.

Equally revealing of the contrast are the divergent Jewish perceptions of their own disabilities and suffering. The Jews of Christendom—hated, oppressed, and frequently physically attacked—poured out their grief in a long string of lachrymose dirges and chronicles that they incorporated into their liturgy. The commemoration of their suffering was branded on the collective Jewish consciousness and was the basis for the so-called "lachrymose" interpretation of Jewish history in modern Jewish historiography. The Jews of Islam, at least in the period under discussion, largely refrained from such exercises of literary woe. The event that evoked Jewish responses most closely approximating the European writings was the terrible persecution, massacre, and forced conversion of Jews and Christians in mid-twelfth-century Spain and North Africa under the Almohades. These include the mournful phrases at the end of the chronicle of rabbinic history by the twelfth-century Spanish-Jewish philosopher Abraham ibn Daud, the doleful Hebrew poem of Abraham ibn Ezra on the destruction of Jewish communities in North Africa, and the litany of cruel suffering by Judah ben Joseph ibn 'Aqnin. These texts bear eloquent witness to the trauma experienced by Jews during those difficult times. It is, indeed, against the background of this unprecedented persecution that Maimonides, himself a refugee from Almohade terror, wrote the lines quoted at the beginning of this essay.

Similarly, as Bernard Septimus has shown,[12] it was apparently the Almohade persecution that gave rise to a new Jewish saying (a purposeful distortion of an ancient midrashic utterance): "Better (to live) under Edom [i.e., Christendom] than under Ishmael [i.e., Islam]." This claim that Christendom provided a more secure home for the Jews than Islam, first made by refugees from Almohade persecution who had found a haven across the border in the Christian kingdoms of Northern Spain, has unknowingly been revived in our own day in the writings of proponents of what I have called here, alternatively, the "counter-myth" of unrelenting Islamic persecution of the Jews, or the "neo-lachrymose" interpretation of Jewish history.

Contemporaries of the Almohade persecution, like Maimonides, perceived that an era of relative security and cultural integration was drawing to a close. Indeed, the later Islamic Middle Ages, from the late twelfth or early thirteenth century on, saw—as even the architects of the myth of the interfaith utopia acknowledged—a steady decline in Jewish fortunes. There were many causes for this reversal, and the process, with its remissions, especially under Ottoman rule in the sixteenth century—a period often called the second "Golden Age" of Jewish life under Islam—is well described in the books by Bernard Lewis and Norman Stillman mentioned above. The extent to which one can speak of a deterioration in the situation of the Jews in later medieval Islam, similar to the position of the Jews in medieval Christendom; the degree to which one can apply the adjective "lachrymose" to the life and history of the Jews of Islam in recent centuries; and the extent to which modern Arab anti-Semitism—modeled in the first instance largely upon Christian stereotypes imported from the West and now nurtured by indigenous Islamic theological hostility—has become an immovable impediment to peaceful rapprochement between Israel and her Arab neighbors, are all matters for further reflection.

*This essay also appears in *The Jerusalem Quarterly* 38 (1986): 125-137, and is reprinted here with the author's permission.

1. Originally 1946; reprint, New York, 1965. See especially pp. 391-392, 410.
2. Paris, 1972.
3. Beirut, 1980.
4. Cairo, n.d., 2: 349-361.
5. Cairo, 1970, 497-505.
6. Some examples: Saul S. Friedlander, "The Myth of Arab Toleration," *Midstream* 16, no. 1 (January, 1970): 56-59; Maurice M. Roumani in collaboration with Deborah Goldman and Helene Korn, "The Persecution of Jews in Arab Lands," in *The Case of the Jews from Arab Countries: A Neglected Issue*, (Jerusalem, 1975), 1: 41-57; Martin Gilbert, *The Jews of Arab Lands: Their History in Maps* (London, 1975); Rose Lewis, "Muslim Grandeur and the Spanish Jews," *Midstream* 23, no. 2 (February, 1977): 26-37; idem, "Maimonides and the Muslims," *Midstream* 25, no. 9 (November, 1979): 16-22; Eliezer Whartman, "Islam vs. the Jews, Zionism and Israel," *Newsview*, 5 July 1983, 12-17.
7. Rutherford, New Jersey, 1985.
8. New York, 1984. The quotation at the end of this paragraph is from page 75.
9. Princeton, 1984.
10. Philadelphia, 1979. The present writer reviewed this book in the *Association for Jewish Studies Newsletter*, no. 28 (March, 1981): 13-14.
11. "The Jews and Islam in the High Middle Ages: A Case of the Muslim View of Difference," in *Gli ebrei nell'alto medioevo* (Spoleto, 1980), 2: 682-683. This paper presents a balanced and well reasoned analysis of the subject. Some of the responses to the paper at the symposium at which it was given, which were published in the volume, betray what we have called here the counter-myth or "neo-lachrymose" trend.
12. "Better under Edom than under Ishmael: The History of a Saying" (in Hebrew), *Zion* 47 (1982): 103-111, with an English summary.

The "Soules Language" in the Song of Songs
by
Michael V. Fox

The book of Proverbs, that strait-laced and solemn book of wise counsels, confesses its amazement at an ancient mystery:

Three things there are too wondrous for me,
four I cannot fathom:
the way of the eagle in the sky,
the way of a snake on a rock,
the way of a ship in the heart of the sea—
and the way of a man with a maid (Prov. 30:18-19).

The way of a man and a maid is a wonder and a mystery, and poets in all ages have delighted in exploring it. What is this peculiar, unseen force that draws the sexes together? How does it feel? How does it affect those in its power? Let us look at the answers to these questions implicit in the Song of Songs' portrayal of love and lovers.

Every literary portrayal creates a world around the characters portrayed. Reading entails reconstructing the world of the poem on the basis of the little piece of that world revealed to us in the text. If we listen carefully to what the characters in a love poem say to each other, we can discern the poet's assumptions and ideas about the ways lovers speak to each other, what they feel, and what they do. We can see the poet's assumptions about the way males and females behave in love, the ways society treats lovers and the way they *feel* society treats them. We have to use the imagination to see these things, but the essence of poetry is that it controls and guides the imagination.

The poet of the Song (as the Song of Songs is often called) does not scrutinize love with a philosopher's eye, attempting to ascertain its essence or cosmic function. The Song speaks of specifics, presenting specific lovers and their feelings, urges, and experiences. But *we* may generalize, looking for the poet's underlying ideas and assumptions about lovers and love.

The concept of love we find in most love songs, the Song of Songs among them, is more likely an ideal of love than a reality. We should beware of the tendency to assume that a poem *describes* the society it is meant to entertain, as well as the tendency to understand a poem as if its characters necessarily behave in accordance with the society's rules. From love poetry we learn how particular writers have perceived love and defined its potentialities, but the poet's view of love need not conform to the picture of social realities we get from other sources.

This essay addresses certain questions frequently asked about Western love poetry but seldom applied to the Song of Songs: (1) To what degree is the lovers' behavior governed by predetermined sex roles? (2) What does sexuality mean to their relationship? (3) How, in the poet's view, does love make lovers speak? and (4) How does love make lovers see? In other words: sex roles, sexuality, speech, and sight.

Society: Sex Roles and Distinctions

In our own day we have become sensitive to the question of sex roles. We are aware that society reaches into even our most private relationships by impressing deeply both in our conscious and in our subconscious patterns of expectations as to how the sexes should and do behave. But how *do* the sexes differ? Beyond the obvious, societies answer this question variously, then try to impose their answers on individuals. Poets too have different answers. Some love poetries, such as the medieval troubadour songs, stress the differences to the extreme, giving the sexes profoundly different and virtually irreconcilable concerns and drives, thus creating for them completely different sets of duties. Such stereotyped sex roles are absent from the Song—surprising indeed, considering how heavily sex roles seem to have weighed on all aspects of life in the ancient world.

Neither lover in the Song is a sexual stereotype. There is only one kind of erotic love in the Song, and the behavior of the sexes in love is fundamentally similar. Each lover invites the other to come away; each goes out at night to find the other; each knows moments of hesitation; each desires sexual fulfillment. The two lovers say similar things to each other, express the same desires and delights, and praise each other in the same ways. Most important, neither feels an asymmetry in the quality or intensity of their emotions, a feeling that would be revealed if, for example, one lover tried to wheedle the reluctant other into love or worried about the steadfastness of the other's affections.

This egalitarian view of love is no deliberate rejection of preordained sex roles, nor are the girl's assertiveness and her equality with her lover a social statement, for she does not imply: although I am a female I will not wait at home but will go out and pursue my love; although I am a female I will seek to satisfy my sexual desires; although I am a female I will brave the night; although I am a female I will not demur at telling my lover how I feel. Such "althoughs" would have to be implied if the girl's forthright assertion of her sexuality were meant as a rejection of a sex role or of a socially imposed stereotype. When the Shulammite bridles at the restrictions placed upon her and insists on her right to love, it is not because of any feeling that females should not thus be restricted, but rather because of her conviction that she is personally sexually mature, whatever anyone else may think (8:10).

Nor do the lovers represent sexual *archetypes*. There is no effort to bring out the essentially female in the Shulammite or the essentially male in the youth. The lovers are two individuals, not type-figures, and they do not have archetypically male or female traits. They differ anatomically, of course, and the girl is spoken of in images implying softness more often than the boy is. But most of the imagery is common to both. The eyes of both are like doves (4:1, 5:12). Both are tall and proud like trees (5:15, 7:8). Parts of both are rounded and crafted like works of art (5:14, 15a; 7:2b, 3a). If she is as lofty as towers or as exalted as the morning star in her lover's eyes, he is as lofty and majestic as the Lebanon in hers. The imagery does not separate the sexes into two fundamentally different types.

Nor does the Song mention or even allude to the most essential of sexual differentia, which is not the external genitalia but the womb. That women alone can bear children is a fact of limitless social, economic, and personal consequence. But this quintessentially female ability, vital for the race and crucial to much individual well-being and happiness, is passed over in silence in the Song. The lovers do not even *muse* about the children they will have together. In the carefully circumscribed horizon of this love poem, anatomy is not destiny.

Yet it is evident that the sexes are not equally free as far as society is concerned. The boy's freedom of movement seems greater: he appears (we never learn from where) and disappears at will. We learn this from her words:

Listen! My beloved—
he's coming now!
Bounding over the mountains,
leaping over the hills (2:8).

The girl is subject to restrictions that her brothers place upon her. Near the beginning of the poem she complains:

> Pay no mind that I am swarthy,
> that the sun has gazed upon me.
> My mother's sons were mean to me,
> made me keeper of the vineyards.
> *My* vineyard I could not keep (1:6).

But these imposed restrictions are an external obstacle, not an inequality within the love relationship. While social realities do impinge upon the world of the poem, *within their one-to-one relationship* the lovers act with equal freedom and express their love in the same ways. But their personalities do differ.

Of the two lovers, the girl appears generally to be the more resolute and zealous in pursuing the fulfillment of their mutual love. They both brave danger. But while he bounds over the mountains at night to visit her—an act whose danger (which in reality might be great) is not mentioned—her risks receive emphasis, as she twice faces the explicit danger of searching for her lover through the city at night, acting in an aberrant way, and being beaten by the night watch. Above all, it is she who makes the proud declaration of love's hard, burning power:

> Place me as a seal upon your heart,
> as a seal upon your arm.
> For love is strong as death,
> jealousy as hard as Sheol.
> Its darts are darts of fire—
> lightning itself!
> Mighty waters cannot extinguish love,
> nor rivers wash it away.
> Should one offer all his estate for love,
> it would be utterly scorned (8:6-7).

Whatever he feels, she is the one we hear proclaiming the power of love, so that we know firsthand that *she* feels love's fire. Thus she appears the tougher, more determined, more vehement lover. She needs these qualities because she is the one who must break through family restrictions and societal expectations and shrug off companions' teasing. In this way the limitations that society places on girls do affect the Shulammite, not by making her a female "type," but by hardening her, forcing her to pursue her goals more obstinately.

Sexuality

Various kinds of sexual pleasures, including coitus, are mentioned or hinted at in the Song of Songs, though just where these allusions are is a matter of inevitable uncertainty. Let us consider more prosaically and less delicately than the Song itself does just what sexual intercourse means to the lovers' relationships.

The lovers in the Song make love in many ways. They caress each other with words of affection, kiss deeply, smell each other's fragrance, lie snuggled in each other's embrace. They "eat" and "drink" love—imbibe it, fill themselves with it, get drunk on it. All the senses partake. The Song does not, however, describe coitus. It alludes to it, sometimes quite transparently, but always as something that will occur beyond the scene. We cannot say for certain just what the lovers are supposed to be doing.

Allusions always maintain some ambiguity, and indeed that is of their essence. Still, the poet of the Song gives us adequate reason to suppose that sexual intercourse is part of the lovers' relationship. The youth spends the night nestled between his beloved's breasts in their garden bower (1:13f.). This scene does not continue through the night, so the audience can only imagine what the couple is likely to do in such circumstances. Later the Shulammite invites her beloved to come away:

> Come, my beloved, let's go to the field.
> We'll pass the night in the countryside:
> we'll go early to the vineyards.
> We'll see if the vine has blossomed,
> the bud opened,
> the pomegranates bloomed.
> There I will give you my love (7:12-13).

"There I will give you my love [my *dodim*]" is close to an explicit declaration that she will have intercourse with him, for *dodim* means sexual lovemaking and usually implies coitus. Elsewhere, when the youth describes his girl as a garden of spices, she invites him into his garden:

> Awake, O north wind, and come, O south!
> Blow on my garden that its spices may flow.
> Let my beloved come into his garden,
> and eat of its luscious fruits (4:16).

At this point another voice urges the lovers to drink their fill of *dodim* (5:1b). There are other phrases that suggest lovemaking of such intensity and intimacy that intercourse is the likely outcome.

This unmistakable eroticism has led some interpreters from most ancient times to assume that the couple is bride and groom, for how else would they dare do such things? Yet a reading unbiased by notions of propriety leaves little doubt that the lovers in the Song are not married or even at their wedding. The girl is still under her brothers' control, or at least they would have it so (1:6). The brothers speak of her betrothal as a future event, "the day when she will be spoken for" (8:8). The lovers' behavior in general is not that of a married couple. No bridegroom or husband would have to sneak up to his wife's house at night, peeking in through the windows, asking to be let in (3:1ff., 5:2ff). Neither (one hopes) would a new bride have to leave her bed at night to chase about the city looking for her husband (ibid.). Nor would a married woman, or even a betrothed woman, have to wish that her beloved were like a brother to her so that she could kiss him openly and bring him home to mother (8:1f). For the Song, sexual intercourse does not consummate marriage. Rather, marriage will consummate sex, placing the stamp of public acceptance upon their union.

This poem is not about married sexuality, but neither is it about mere dalliance. The lovers are intensely serious about their love and fully committed to each other. The Song is a poem about a love that—as the lovers see it—will inevitably lead to marriage and continue throughout their lives, for nothing but death can match its power. But the lovers are so intent upon the present moment that they do not think of anything beyond the wedding, and they give little thought even to that. This nearly exclusive focus on the immediate experience gives their love, for all its seriousness, an adolescent quality—as indeed it should, for they are adolescents, blossoming with the land and scarcely aware of anything beyond the springtime of their lives.

The Song does assume a sexual ethic, but the sexual virtue cherished is not chastity. It is fidelity: unquestioned devotion to one's lover, a devotion that can make one risk the anger of family, the teasing of peers, the violence of society's guardians, and the dangers of the night to reach and unite with one's lover. It is a love that binds lovers together as closely and constantly as a seal upon the heart and arm and that makes one as vehemently possessive as the grave, which gets what it wants and holds it forever.

Speech: Communication between Lovers

The Song of Songs is true dialogue throughout. Even in passages that have the appearance of monologue because one of the personae speaks alone for a relatively long time, there is always a listener within the poem. It is usually clear that the lovers are speaking and listening to each other. Furthermore, they *influence* each other through speech: they respond to what they hear. What each says and does depends in large part on what the other says.

Often one lover responds directly to a request or hint given by the other. For example, in 4:12-14 the youth describes his beloved as a garden of spices:

> A garden locked is my sister, my bride . . .
> spikenard and saffron, cane and cinnamon,
> with frankincense trees of all kinds,
> myrrh and aloes,
> with all the best spices.

She picks up the hint and invites him in:

> Awake, O north wind, and come, O south!
> Blow on my garden that its spices may flow.
> Let my beloved come into his garden,
> and eat of its luscious fruits (4:16).

And he accepts:

> I come into my garden, my sister, my bride.
> I taste my myrrh with my spice . . . (5:1).

Such feedback in communication is so frequent that its function in conveying the reciprocity of love is easily overlooked. The poet further brings out the interaction of the lovers and establishes the reciprocity of their communication by the use of *echoing*, in which the words of one lover are patterned on the other's and thus recall them.

Their words intertwine closely in the rapid exchange in 2:1-3a. The girl begins:

> *ani havatzelet ha-sharon,*
> *shoshanat ha-amakim*
> I'm just a crocus of Sharon,
> a valley-lily.

Self praise would be pointless here; rather, this is a modest self-appraisal: I'm just one among myriads. The point of this mild self-deprecation can only be to fish for praise and reassurance. To this her lover immediately responds by turning her own words to use in praising her pre-eminence:

ke-shoshanah bein ha-hohim
kein rayati bein ha-banot
Like a lily among brambles,
so is my darling among girls.

She in turn patterns her praise of him on *his* words, likewise declaring him one of a kind:

ke-tapuah ba-atzei ha-ya'ar
kein dodi bein ha-banim
Like an apricot tree among trees of the thicket,
so is my beloved among boys.

Their words are even more closely interlocked in 7:10. The boy says, continuing his Praise Song:

ve-hikekh ke-yein ha-tov
and your palate [is] like the best wine . . .

The girl completes his sentence by turning the compliment into an offer of the sweetness of her mouth:

holeikh le-dodi le-meisharim
doveiv siftei [shanim]
flowing smoothly to my beloved,
dripping on scarlet lips.

There are numerous examples of echoing. In particular, the rapidity of the exchanges where the words of the two lovers are closely intertwined makes us feel that the lovers are highly sensitive to each other, that the words of one quickly impress themselves on the heart and mind of the other. The alacrity of their response gives their expressions of love and desire a tone of exhilaration and urgency. The communication of these lovers is more than transmission of thoughts. It is *communion*, intimate and reciprocal influence through language. The words of each lover penetrate the other's thought and speech. Love in the Song is thus the interinanimation of two souls, as John Donne defined love's essence. In fact, Donne's love poetry in many ways parallels the view of love implicit in the Song:

> If any, so by love refin'd
> That he soules language understood
> And by good love were growen all minde,
> Within convenient distance stoode,
> He (though he knew not which soule spake,
> Because both meant, both spake the same)
> Might thence a new concoction take
> And part farre purer then he came.
>   *The Extasie*

And indeed, the meshing and echoing of the lovers' words in the Song does produce a "new concoction," one not reducible to the sum of each lover's statements.

Love as Vision

As well as reaching into feelings and relationships, love affects perception: lovers *see* things differently from others. Lovers' vision is at the very heart of the Song's concern: the lovers' descriptions of the world about them show how they see each other, and their descriptions of each other show how they see the world.

Their thoughts and conversations concentrate almost entirely on what they see and feel right now. Love is not blind, but young lovers do have tunnel vision. They see nothing but each other and care little about anything but the immediate experience. This narrowness of vision gives their romance an adolescent quality—what an outside observer might call "infatuation."

The lovers project their feelings onto the world they see about them. When they look at the blossoming countryside, they sense in nature the same lush, erotic efflorescence that they feel within themselves. The sensuousness of nature becomes a correlative of the sensuousness of love. In particular the girl's experience of sexuality has its counterpart in nature, for the Song is first of all the song of her sexual blossoming. The lovers describe the blossoming of the land in spring (2:10-13, 7:13-14), but at the same time they sense in it the blossoming of the girl. She herself is a vineyard (1:6, 8:12), which, now that it is being tended, is blossoming, or, perhaps, now that it is blossoming, is being tended. She is a garden with sweet fruits and fragrant spices, an orchard with pomegranates and choice fruits (4:12-16). She will let him drink the juice of her pomegranate (8:2b), which is surely her breast, now ripe.

The lovers' description of the countryside in spring is so sensual because they see—and smell, and hear, and taste—their beloved in the world about them. They also see, smell, hear, and taste the world in their beloved.

The nature of lovers' perception is best revealed in the passages in the Song where one lover praises the other part by part (4:1-7, 4:9-15, 5:10-16, 6:4-10, and 7:2-10a). The imagery of these passages, which are known as "praise songs," is impressive and intriguing, yet at the same time difficult and foreign, perhaps the most foreign aspect of the Song for the modern reader. Yet it is this imagery above all that reveals to us the poet's view of a lover's perception.

In the Praise Songs description is rare, and the metaphors offer little information about how the lovers look, often seeming actually to interfere with the formation of a mental picture of them. Many images are startling:

Your nose is like the tower of Lebanon,
looking toward Damascus (7:5b).

Your navel is a rounded bowl—
may it never lack mixed wine! (7:3a).

His belly is an ivory bar,
adorned with lapis lazuli (5:14b).

In such metaphors, the poet maintains a "metaphoric distance"—an unexpectedness or incongruity—between image and referent, yet bridges that distance by making us see each part of the body in terms of the image. The poet's strategy is to point us to each part of the lovers' bodies as if describing it, then to set before our eyes images that cannot comfortably be assimilated to their referents, the parts of the body that are spoken of. This dislocation of expectations directs our attention to the images themselves rather than to the parts of the body. The images, not quickly serving the task that seems to have been laid upon them, become independent of their referents and memorable in themselves. In other words, what do you remember more vividly after having read the Song—a boy and a girl who look a certain way, or black goats filing down a distant mountainside, perky young gazelle twins, heaps of wheat hedged by lilies, and so on? For me it is the imagery itself that makes the sharpest, most enduring impression, and I think that this is the author's intention.

As the poem proceeds, the images, given an importance independent of their referents, combine to form a cohesive picture of a self-contained world: a peaceful, fruitful world, resplendent with the blessings of nature and the beauties of human art. That world blossoms in a perpetual spring. Doves hide shyly, sit near water channels, and bathe in milk. Spices give forth their fragrance. Springs flow with clear water. Fruits and wines offer their sweetness. Mounds of wheat are surrounded by lilies. Ewes, white and clean, bear twins and never miscarry. Goats stream gently down the mountainside. Proud and ornate towers stand tall above the landscape. Nor are there lacking silver and gold, precious stones, and objects of art: a rich and blessed world.

This world provides a harmonious backdrop to the expressions of love. Far more important, it also reveals the author's idea of the way a lover views the world. It is a *psychological* reality that the poet discloses. The point is not the beloved's beauty (which, strictly speaking, the *poet* never asserts, for all the praise is spoken by one of the lovers), but rather what a lover perceives in and through this beauty. The imagery of the praise thus shows us not how the lovers *look*, but how they *see*. Lovers look at each other and, through the prism of physical form, see an ever-present Arcady. The eroticism of the Praise Songs thus transcends physical beauty. The imagery is inadequate as physical description because the lovers are not seeing physical features so much as looking *through* them to materializations of their own emotion. Furthermore, since that world comes into being and is unified only through the lovers' perception of each other, the imagery reveals a *new* world—one *created* by love.

Lovers see each other as unique. In the Praise Songs they say: my lover is like no other lover, my love is like no other love, my world is fresh and new and charged with a strange loveliness. Literal physical descriptions or standard, easily grasped tropes would not convey this freshness of vision, whereas the peculiar, surprising images in which the lovers in the Song speak of each other do indeed do so. The poet puts bold, unexpected images into a traditional pattern, creating metaphors that stretch our imaginations by maintaining a distance between what is spoken of and what is said about it. In this way we can join in the excitement of discovery as the lovers discover a new world in each other.

Love in the Song of Songs is not only an emotion: it is also a confluence of souls, best expressed by tightly interlocking dialogue; and it is a mode of perception, best communicated through the imagery of praise. Love is a communion in which lovers look at each other with an intensely concentrated vision that broadens to elicit a world of its own. For the Song, love is a way of seeing—and creating—a world, a private, idyllic universe. A similar view of love was well articulated by John Donne throughout his love poetry. On the power of love over perception Donne said:

> For love, all love of other sights controules,
> And makes one little roome, an every where,
> . . . . .
> Let us possesse one world, each hath one, and is one.
> *The Good Morrow*

And further: "So we shall be one, and one another's All" (*"Lovers Infiniteness"*).

Or, in the words of Genesis:
ve-hayu le-vasar ehad
and they shall become one flesh.

Attitudes of the Kabbalists and Hasidim Towards Maimonides
by
Louis Jacobs

The kabbalists and the hasidim had what we would call today "a love-hate relationship" with Maimonides. On the one hand, Maimonides' halakhic views were totally accepted as a major contribution to the halakhic process, and there were strong affinities between some of his theological positions and theirs. On the other hand, some of Maimonides' theological opinions were in direct contradiction with the Kabbalah. In this essay we can note both the affinities and the contradictions between Maimonides and these mystics.

It is now generally acknowledged that to describe Maimonides as a "rationalist" for whom, in the language of Ahad Ha-Am,[1] reason was supreme, is mistaken. Maimonides, for all his emphasis on the role of human reasoning, can qualify as a mystic. The man who could speak of the soul love-sick for God[2] and who developed the idea of *devekut*, cleaving to God in mind and heart, in a way almost parallel to the mystics,[3] was poles removed from the sober rationalist of convention. The extremely rare individual, says Maimonides,[4] who had God always in his thoughts, can walk unharmed through fire and water. Heschel has shown that Maimonides even believed that he had attained to the lower degrees of prophecy![5] It would seem that the doctrine of *devekut* in Hasidism—in which the idea occupied a central place—owes much, in fact, to the formulation of the ideal in Maimonides, although this was not always frankly admitted.[6]

Secondly, the kabbalists, concerned to have their doctrines (grossly anthropomorphic on the surface) understood in a refined way—they repeatedly stressed that their mythical description of the *sefirot* referred to purely spiritual associations and that *hagshamah* ("corporeality") was heretical—welcomed the *via negativa* of the philosophers in general and Maimonides in particular. With regard to the kabbalistic doctrine of *En Sof*—God as He is in Himself—the kabbalists went beyond Maimonides' notion of negative attributes,[7] declaring that of *En Sof* nothing whatsoever can be said, no human thought is capable of grasping this aspect of the Deity.[8] The suggestion that God really did appear to the prophets in the guise of a king, sitting on His throne and surrounded by His angels, only seems preposterous to Jews because of the efforts of Maimonides and the other philosophers. In the thirteenth century, the anthropomorphic picture was accepted by many of the distinguished traditionalists, as we learn from the *Ketav Tamim* of Moses of Taku, who thought that Maimonides and his colleagues were advancing a new religion as a substitute for Judaism, and from the objection of Abraham ibn David of Posquieres (ca. 1125-1195) to Maimonides' declaration that anyone who believes that God is corporeal is a heretic.[9]

The famous Safed kabbalist Moses Cordovero (1522-1570) writes: "All that has been written by those who pursue the knowledge of God through human reasoning in the matter of the divine nature is totally correct in negating from His being the attributes and actions."[10] In his *Pardes Rimmonim*,[11] Cordovero accepts Maimonides' statement[12] that in God Knower, Knowledge and the Known is all One. Cordovero is followed in this by the most systematic hasidic thinker, Sheneur Zalman of Liady (1747-1813), founder of the *Habad* trend in Hasidism.[13] Sheneur Zalman's grandson, Menahem Mendel of Lubavitch (1789-1866), in his *Derekh Mitzvotekha*,[14] has a lengthy treatment of Maimonides' negative attributes, stressing its affinity with the Kabbalah.

On the debit side, a number of Maimonides' statements were anathema to the kabbalists. A major source of offense, for them as for the anti-Maimonists, was Maimonides' identification of the rabbinic *Ma'aseh Bereshit* ("Work of Creation") and *Ma'aseh Merkavah* ("Work of the Heavenly Chariot") with Aristotelian "physics" and "metaphysics."[15] This was, for the kabbalists, to reduce the "mysteries of the Torah," its inner soul, to exercises in Greek science and philosophy. In the attack by Shem Tov ibn Shem Tov (ca. 1380-1441) on Maimonides' views, this kabbalist scornfully remarks: "Heaven forbid that we should understand it in this way. If that were so then these mysteries are available to all, to the pure and the impure, to the believer and the heretic, to the Canaanite, Hittite, Amonite and Moabite."[16]

Maimonides' mighty attempt to give reasons for the precepts of the Torah[17] was held to be futile by the kabbalists. For them, the *mitzvot* had an effect on the worlds on high, each detail corresponding to this or that spiritual entity, instead of which Maimonides supplies reasons which make the *mitzvot* into a means to social, ethical (or, even, religious) ends but which, by implication, have no intrinsic value. As Shem Tov ibn Shem Tov puts it: "And when the rabbi [Maimonides] comes to provide reasons for the commandments, the truth be told, no one will discover any *mitzvah* to be carried out for its own purpose. Either it is for the purpose of nullifying nonsensical opinions, as are [for Maimonides] all the laws regarding idolatry and its worship, the sacrificial system, the Temple, its vessels and those who minister there, and to affirm God's unity; or for the purpose of controlling the appetites, as are the forbidden foods and sexual relationships and other *mitzvot*; or it is for the purpose of improving the character, as are charity, tithing, the poorman's gifts, the laws of damages and of monetary claims; or for the purpose of remembering the creation of the world or the unity of God."[18]

The kabbalist Isaac of Acre (13th-14th cent.), in his *Meirat Einayim*,[19] admires Maimonides' attempt at refining the God idea and Maimonides' mystical fervor, but finds the sage's attitude towards the reasons for the *mitzvot* unworthy of him. "Although the words of the *Guide for the Perplexed* refine the mind and direct the intellect aright, bringing those who understand his ideas correctly to a comprehension of the Creator, to love Him with a perfect, untainted love, with a whole heart and a soul filled with desire, as Scripture says: 'Know thou the God of thy father, and serve Him with a whole heart and with a willing mind' (I Chron. 28:9), yet in connection with the reasons for the *mitzvot* he said nothing at all adequate but as one who tries to push away an adversary with a straw."

The kabbalists also shared in the opposition by the traditionalists to Maimonides' eschatological view; his identification of the World to Come with the immortality of the soul;[20] his belief that it is only the "acquired soul," the soul gained through metaphysical speculation, that is immortal;[21] and his apparent rejection of the doctrine of Hell, equating it with annihilation of the sinful soul, not with torment.[22]

With Maimonides' view of angels[23] as entirely disembodied spirits who could never appear in human form, the kabbalists, with their rich angelology, based on the rabbinic literature, could hardly be in sympathy. Nahmanides (1195-1270), great talmudist, kabbalist and admirer of Maimonides, is horrified at the suggestion that all the biblical references to angels appearing as human refers to appearance in a dream, so that Jacob did not really wrestle with the angel, Sarah and Abraham were not actually visited by angels; it was all a dream, as was the episode of Balaam and the ass.[24]

Maimonides also angered the kabbalists in his silence on the whole doctrine of the *sefirot*, so central to the kabbalistic scheme, of which he appeared to be ignorant. On Maimonides' philosophical understanding of Moses seeking God's back but not His face (Exodus 33:20),[25] Abraham ibn David remarks: "Face and Back is a great mystery, which it is improper to reveal to everyone. Perhaps the author of this statement did not know it."[26]

Few of the kabbalists saw fit to denigrate Maimonides in the manner of Shem Tov ibn Shem Tov. Moses Alashkar (1466-1552) appends to his responsa collection[27] a lengthy attack on Shem Tov and a defense of Maimonides, though, in the process, he makes Maimonides more conventional than he really is and goes so far as to make him a convert to the Kabbalah, as we shall see. Shem Tov's sons and grandson did not share his rejection of Maimonides. On the contrary, they were followers of many of Maimonides' views. It is one of the ironies of the whole debate that Shem Tov's grandson, also called Shem Tov, compiled one of the standard commentaries to Maimonides' *Guide of the Perplexed*.[28] Yet we learn from the *Maggid Mesharim* of Joseph Caro (1488-1575) that, in the sixteenth century, some kabbalists had a very unflattering view of Maimonides.

The *Maggid Mesharim* is the mystical diary kept by Caro, like Maimonides a great lawyer and mystic, in which his "Maggid," a visitant from the upper worlds, communicated messages to him. The very revealing communication referring to Maimonides reads: "When you die the Rambam of blessed memory will come out to meet you because you solved the difficulties in his Code of Laws. He belongs among the saints, not, as those sages say, that he was reincarnated as a worm. For let it be that it was so decreed, because of words of his he spoke improperly, yet his Torah learning protected him and also his good deeds of which he was a master. He was never reincarnated as a worm. He was obliged to suffer reincarnation [in some other form] but when he departed that life he was admitted into the realm of the saints."[29]

Nahman of Bratzlav (1772-1811), hasidic leader and opponent of the Haskalah movement, centuries later, is the most outspoken mystic of all against Maimonides' philosophical views as being incompatible with mystic faith.[30] Whoever studies Maimonides' *Guide*, says Rabbi Nahman, destroys the holy image of God, and as for the reasons Maimonides gives for such precepts as the sacrificial cult and incense,[31] they are all nonsense. Horodesky was told by a Bratzlaver hasid of the bold statement by Nahman: "There are many thinkers whom the world treats as great men, especially the Rambam. But in the future world they will know that he was an unbeliever and a heretic!"[32]

Among the majority of the kabbalists, admiration for Maimonides gained the upper hand and the inevitable happened: Maimonides was himself turned into a kabbalist, albeit a secret one. The first mention of this is in the commentary to Maimonides' Code, *Migdal Oz*, by Shem Tov ibn Gaon (13th-14th cent.). Ibn Gaon composed the work some time after he had emigrated from his native Spain to Palestine in 1312. He is commenting on the passage, mentioned above, where Abraham ibn David supposes that Maimonides was not an initiate into the mysteries of the Kabbalah.[33] Maimonides' explanation, says Ibn Gaon, of Face and Back does, indeed, pursue the philosophical approach but that does not mean he was unaware of the Kabbalah, as Ibn David suggests. Ibn Gaon continues: "In my opinion Maimonides, of blessed memory, did come to know the Kabbalah towards the end of his life. For I hereby testify that I saw in Spain my birthplace a very old begrimed parchment scroll in which was written: 'I, Moshe ben R. Maimon, reflected on the subject of the end of days, after I had descended into the halls of the Chariot.' What he says here is very close to the ideas of the kabbalists to which our great teacher, Nahmanides, of blessed memory, alludes at the beginning of his *Commentary to the Torah*."[34]

The legend of Maimonides' conversion to the Kabbalah received further elaboration after the expulsion from Spain. Evidently, the collapse of Spanish Jewry and its philosophical tendencies encouraged the kabbalists to win Maimonides over to their ranks. Meir ibn Gabbai (1486-after 1540) wrote his classical work on the Kabbalah, *Avodat Ha-Kodesh*, in the years 1523-1531. Here he writes:

> Who was greater in philosophical expertise than the Rambam, of blessed memory? Yet once he had found the pearl he threw away the pebbles. One of the true sages [i.e. a kabbalist], who explained the mysteries of the Ramban,[35] writes as follows in his commentary to *Beshalach*. "This man, Rabbi Jacob, went to Egypt to transmit the Kabbalah to the Rambam, of blessed memory. So overjoyed was he [Maimonides] that he praised it [the Kabbalah] to his disciples. However, he did not have this privilege until the latter days of his life, when he had composed all the works of his we have today." The sage, Rabbi Isaac Abravanel, of blessed memory, in his work *Nahalat Avot*, writes as follows, at the end of chapter "Akavia,"[36] "I, too, have heard that the great rabbi, Maimonides, wrote, 'Towards the end of my life a certain person came to me saying to me tasty words. Were it not for the fact that this was towards the end of my life, when my works had been published throughout the world, I would have retracted many of the things I had recorded therein.' And there is no doubt that it was the Kabbalah about which he had heard towards the end of his days." He [Abravanel] only heard it as a report. But I have actually seen a work in which it is stated in his [Maimonides'] name: "Towards the end of my life a certain venerable sage came to me and he illumined my eyes in the kabbalistic science. Were it not for the fact that my works have been published, I would have retracted many of the things I have written therein."[37]

This alleged secret document is referred to in Moses Alashkar's defense of Maimonides referred to above. In his reply to Shem Tov ibn Shem Tov's denial that Maimonides knew the Kabbalah, Alashkar writes:

> First of all, I must record the words of the Rabbi [Maimonides], of blessed memory, which he wrote to his beloved disciple, in a secret document regarding the profound mysteries of the true Kabbalah.... "For most of my days I was perplexed[38] about the investigation of

existing things to know their true meaning, according to the methods of the philosophers and by means of logical postulates. But it now seems that these methods are at fault, at least. For that which was obvious to them [the philosophers] had not been proven by any disproof of the contrary.[39]... But the practitioners of the true Kabbalah, by methods assured against error, are able to comprehend all matters capable of comprehension quite easily. It was by these methods that the prophets proceeded, comprehending all they did, knowing the future and carrying out strange acts of a supernatural order. I also took to myself some few of these methods for the investigation of the nature of things and all my doubts were stilled."[40]

And so the legend grew. Joseph Solomon Delmedigo (1591-1655), in his work in defense of the Kabbalah, *Matzref le-Hokhmah*, a reply to the rejection of the Kabbalah by his kinsman, Elijah ben Moses Delmedigo, *Behinat Ha-Dat*,[41] repeats[42] the legend, quoting all the above sources, which, for him, appear conclusive evidence of the authenticity of the report that Maimonides became a kabbalist in his old age and retracted his former opinions. None of these writers appear to be aware that in the process they are accusing Maimonides of subterfuge, of refusing to retract his opinions except in a secret document!

On the other hand, the famous kabbalist Hayyim Vital (1542-1620) appears to have rejected the legend, if he knew of it in the first place. In a mystical vein Vital remarks[43] that both Maimonides and Nahmanides were named "Moses" because their souls were derived from "corners of the head of the Lesser Countenance."[44] But Nahmanides' soul came from the right side and hence he was privileged to know the Kabbalah, whereas Maimonides' soul came from the left side and he was denied knowledge of the Kabbalah. The *"Hida,"* Hayyim Joseph David Azulai (1724-1806), in his biographical note on Maimonides,[45] quotes this saying of Vital and notes that it contradicts the legend. *"Hida"* is obliged to say either that the legend is false or that all Maimonides attained in his old age was how to use the divine names for magical purposes, not the knowledge of the kabbalistic mysteries.

The kabbalist Joseph Ergas (1685-1730) is similarly circumspect. In reply to the accusation that the Kabbalah cannot be an authentic tradition since it was unknown to Maimonides, Ergas[46] suggests a number of possibilities. First, no single person can know everything. Even a Maimonides may have been ignorant of the Kabbalah without this fact causing us to cast aspersions on the science. Secondly, Maimonides may well have known the Kabbalah but in his honesty, as he saw it, he may have rejected the science as he undoubtedly did with regards to such things as belief in demons and magic.[47] Finally, Ergas falls back on the authenticity of the secret document quoted by Alashkar and states that he, himself, has a copy of this very document in his possession. The mystery has deepened.

In the hasidic movement the same ambivalent attitude towards Maimonides' philosophical (though not, of course, his halakhic) views prevailed. In one area in particular, that of divine providence, Maimonides' views were in direct conflict with those of Hasidism. Hasidic immanentism or panentheism[48] refused to allow, as Maimonides held, that God's providence extends only in general to the species other than the human.[49] Hasidism depended for its whole system on the belief that there is individual divine providence for all things in creation. Strangely enough Ergas in his *Shomer Emunim*[50] follows Maimonides on general versus particular providence. Isaac Stern, the editor of the *Shomer Emunim*, lists a number of hasidic masters who took issue with Maimonides and Ergas on this issue.[51] For them every blade of grass lies where it does and in that particular way by a direct divine fiat.[52] Typical is the attitude of Rabbi Hayyim Halberstam of Zans (1791-1876), an admirer of Maimonides. (The hasidim report that the Zanser would study the *Guide of the Perplexed* after Kol Nidre on Yom Kippur and would pray to God that he might be as God-fearing as Maimonides.[53]) Halberstam writes in affirmation of the doctrine of particular providence: "Even though the Rambam, of blessed memory, has a different opinion in this matter, the truth is, as the Rabbis of blessed memory say,[54] that not even a bird is caught in a snare without direct providence from on high, as is well-known."[55]

Hasidism, then, went its own way without being bothered too much as to whether or not its doctrines were compatible with those of Maimonides. A few of the hasidic masters shared Nahman of Bratzlav's hostility to Maimonides' thought. The majority respected Maimonides as a great teacher but refused to study his philosophical ideas. Typical of the compromise position is the story told to Heschel about Menahem Mendel of Kotzk (1787-1859).[56] The Seer of Lublin advised the Kotzker to study Maimonides' Code but to skip the opening chapters, which contain his philosophical views. The Kotzker, however, did not skip these passages but he read them in a cursory fashion without any deep study.

A fairly reliable report[57] tells of the hasidic master Abraham Jacob of Sadegora (1819-1883) repeating a defense of Maimonides by his father Israel of Ruzhyn (1797-1850). The Ruzhyner asked his hasidim, why do people speak ill of Maimonides? Why should they not, exclaimed a rabbi present, since he dares to suggest that Aristotle knew more about mundane matters than the prophet Ezekiel? The Ruzhyner replied: Aristotle was so dazzled by the splendors of the world—the king's palace—that he devoted all his talents to its investigation, whereas Ezekiel was too much dedicated to the king himself to spend time on examining the glories of the palace. Maimonides was right. After telling this, Rabbi Abraham Jacob went on to say that Maimonides was of the seed of David and codified the Law so that all should be ready for the coming of the Messiah, and he himself should have been the Messiah were it not that the world was not ready for his coming. That is why all the righteous try their utmost to defend Maimonides against his detractors. From a foe of the Kabbalah Maimonides has become the longed-for Messiah who was unfortunate enough to be born before his time.

1. Ahad Ha-Am, "Shilton Ha-Sekhel" in *Al Parashat Derakhim* (Berlin, 1921), 4: 1-37. Also see Solomon Goldman, *The Jew and the Universe* (New York, 1936; ed. Anna Pom, New York, 1973), which contains a critique of Ahad Ha-Am's essay on Maimonides.
2. Maimonides, *Mishneh Torah,*"Sefer ha-Mada, Yesodei Ha-Torah" 4:12 and "Hilkhot Teshuvah" 10:3.
3. See Gershom Scholem, "Devekut, or Communion with God" in *The Messianic Idea in Judaism* (New York, 1973), 203-227. On p. 205 Scholem notes the strong resemblances between Maimonides' view of *devekut* and that of the early kabbalist and talmudist, Nahmanides. Nahmanides' statement is in his commentary to Deuteronomy 11:22, *Commentary to the Torah*, ed. H. D. Chavel (Jerusalem, 1960), "Devarim," 395.
4. In his discussion of *devekut*, *Guide*, III, 51.
5. Abraham Joshua Heschel, "Did Maimonides strive for Prophetic Inspiration?" in the *Louis Ginzberg Jubilee Volume*, Heb. section (New York, 1945), 150-188.
6. See Jacob I. Dienstag: "Maimonides' *Guide* and *Sefer HaMadda* in Hasidic Literature" in the *Abraham Weiss Jubilee Volume*, Heb. section (New York, 1964), 307-330. See especially pp. 314-316, where Dienstag provides an illuminating parallel between Maimonides on *devekut* and Abraham of Kalisk (1740-1810).
7. *Guide*, I, 51-60.
8. The Mystical Prayer of Elijah in *Tikkunei Zohar*, Second Introduction.
9. For Abraham Ibn David (Raabad), see his stricture to Maimonides' *Mishneh Torah*, "Teshuvah" 3:7. On Moses of Taku see *Ketav Tamim*, ed. from the Paris manuscript by J. Dan, "Kuntresim," *Texts and Studies* 61 (1984).
10. *Shiur Komah* (Warsaw, 1885) 34b (Arabic no. 67).
11. Chap. 7, "Shaar Mahut ve-Hanhagah" (Jerusalem, 1962).
12. *Mishneh Torah*, "Yesodei Ha-Torah" 2:10; *Guide*, I, 68.
13. *Tanya* (Vilna, 1930), Part I, chaps. 2 and 48; Part II, chap. 7. On this author's discussion of Maimonides' doctrine of negative attributes, see his *Likkutei Torah* (Brooklyn, 1976), "Pikkudei," 6c (Arabic no. 12).
14. *Derekh Mitzvotekha* (Brooklyn, 1976), 46b-47a.
15. *Mishneh Torah*, "Yesodei Ha-Torah" 4:10-13; *Guide*, Introduction.
16. *Sefer Ha-Emunot* (Ferrara, 1556; photo-copy, Jerusalem, 1969), Introduction, 4a.
17. *Guide*, III.
18. *Sefer Ha-Emunot*, I, chap. 1, 7a.
19. Ed. H. A. Erlanger (Jerusalem, 1975), 203.
20. *Mishneh Torah*, "Teshuvah" 8:2.
21. *Guide*, I, 70.
22. *Mishneh Torah*, "Teshuvah" 8:5. For the kabbalistic opposition to Maimonides' eschatology see, e.g., Raabad to "Teshuvah" 8:2, 4; Shem Tov, *Sefer Ha-Emunot*, I, 1, p. 5b; *Migdal Oz* to these passages in the *Mishneh Torah*. *Midrash Ha-Neelam*, Zohar 2, 135b-136a, appears to be based on Maimonides!
23. *Guide*, II, 42.
24. Nahmanides' *Commentary* to Genesis 18:1, ed. Chavel, pp. 103-107.
25. *Mishneh Torah*, "Yesodei Ha-Torah" 1:10.
26. Quoted in *Kesef Mishneh* ad loc., obviously referring to the doctrine of the *sefirot*; perhaps "Face" is *Tiferet* and "Back" is *Malkhut*, or "Face" is *Hesed* and "Back" is *Gevurah*.

27. Jerusalem, 1957, no. 117.
28. E.g., in Lemberg ed. of the *Guide*, 1866.
29. See R. J. Z. Werblowsky, *Joseph Karo: Lawyer and Mystic* (Oxford, 1962), 31 and 170 note 2. Cf. my *Jewish Mystical Testimonies* (New York, 1977), 115-116. Werblowsky points out that the reference to reincarnation in a worm has been omitted from the printed versions of the *Maggid Mesharim* out of respect for Maimonides. Werblowsky supplies it from the manuscript.
30. See Dienstag, op. cit., pp. 316-317.
31. *Shivhei Ha-Ran* (Lemberg, 1864), chapter on: "Keeping Away from Speculation and being strong in Faith."
32. S. A. Horodesky, *Ha-Hasidut ve-Ha-Hasidim* (Berlin, 1923), 2: 40.
33. In *Kesef Mishneh*, to "Yesodei Ha-Torah" 1:10.
34. *Migdal Oz* to *Mishneh Torah,* "Yesodei Ha-Torah" 1:10.
35. On the whole subject of Maimonides' alleged conversion to Kabbalism see the famous essay of G. Scholem, "Me-Hoker li-Mekkubal," *Sefer Ha-Rambam, Tarbiz* 6, no. 3 (1935): 90-98. Scholem notes that it would seem that the author of these commentaries to Ramban is Isaac of Acre in his *Me'irat Einayim,* but Scholem was unable to discover any reference to the report in any of the manuscripts of the work he consulted. It is not found in the Erlanger ed., op. cit., either. Israel Weinstock, *Be-Ma'agalei Ha-Nigleh ve-Ha-Nistar* (Jerusalem, 1969), has adduced a good deal of evidence to show that some of the basic kabbalistic ideas were known to the medieval philosophers including Maimonides. In the light of his investigations, he remarks, the whole question of Maimonides' relationship to the Kabbalah will need to be reopened (118, n. 34). Cf. H. J. Michael, *Or Ha-Hayyim* (Frankfurt, 1891), 537 and 551-2; S. N. Hones, *Toledot Ha-Posekim* (Warsaw, 1922), 443 (from Michael).
36. Opening word of chapter three of *Avot*. In the Jerusalem, 1970, ed. of *Nahalat Avot*, the passage is found on p. 209.
37. *Avodat Ha-Kodesh* (Jerusalem, 1973), Part II, chap. 13, 33c (Arabic no. 66).
38. Heb. *navukh*, obviously inspired by Maimonides *Moreh Nevukhim* (Guide of the Perplexed).
39. The meaning appears to be that the propositions of the philosophers were only guesswork since they had not advanced the convincing proof that the contrary of the positions is false.
40. *Responsa,* op. cit., no. 117, p. 313.
41. *Behinat Ha-Dat*, ed. Isaac Reggio (Vienna, 1833). On p. 40 the older Delmedigo says that none of the geonim knew the Kabbalah. Reggio's note to this page refers to the younger Delmedigo's defense but dismisses it, referring to Leon da Modena (1571-1648), who, in his *Ari Nohem*, ed. Julius Furst (Leipzig, 1840), chap. 12, p. 34, says the whole thing is only a dream.
42. Joseph Solomon Delmedigo (*Yashar* of Candia), *Matzref le-Hokhmah*, ed. D. Tors (Odessa, 1864), 34a-b (Arabic no. 68-69).
43. *Sefer Ha-Gilgulim* (Premisla, 1875), Part II, 8b.
44. *Zeer*, i.e., *Zeer Anpin*, one of the *partzufim* of the Lurianic Kabbalah. Interestingly enough Vital says here that Maimonides did not know the Kabbalah at all whereas Nahmanides came to know it *in his old age.* There seems to be some confusion here between Nahmanides and Maimonides, i.e., the notion that Maimonides only became a Kabbalist in his old age was transferred to Nahmanides.

45. *Shem Ha-Gedolim* (Warsaw, 1876), s.v. "Ha-Rambam," I, no. 100. Azulai refers to the strong doubts expressed as to the authenticity of the secret document in Moses ben Jacob's *Shushin Sodot*, Koretz, 1784, p. 31a.

46. *Shomer Emunim*, ed. Isaac Stern (Jerusalem, 1965), Part I, 12-13, pp. 10-13. The "secret document" is also referred to in the commentary to the *Guide* by Moses b. Joshua of Narbonne (d. 1362): *Narboni*, ed. J. Goldenthal (Vienna, 1852), Part 2, 21, p. 4a.

47. E.g. in *Mishneh Torah*, "Abodah Zarah" 11 end, on magic. *Commentary to Mishnah*, "Abodah Zarah," chap. 4; *Guide*, III, 46 on demons. Cf. *Mishneh Torah*, "Sanhedrin" 12:2, where Maimonides says, "Even if he heard the voice of the one who gave the warning without actually seeing him," obviously giving his interpretation to *Me'ilah* 6b, "even by a demon." See Meiri to *Me'ilah* 6b, who says *derekh mashal*, ("as a parable"; "in a manner of speaking"). Also see Raabad to *Mishneh Torah* ad loc. And see Vilna Gaon to *Yoreh Deah* 179, note 13.

48. See my *Seeker of Unity* (London, 1966).

49. *Guide*, III, 17-18.

50. *Shomer Emunim*, Part I, 81, although Ergas does not mention Maimonides here by name.

51. Stern's Introduction, 31-34.

52. Phinehas of Koretz (1726-1791) in *Peer Layesharim*, ed. I. D. Ozenstein (Jerusalem, 1921). No. 38, p. 5b.

53. Dienstag, op. cit., 325.

54. See Tosafists to *Avodah Zarah* 17b, s.v. "dimos."

55. *Divrei Hayyim* (Brooklyn, 1962), "Mikketz," 13d (Arabic no. 26).

56. See Heschel's Yiddish book *Kotzk* (Tel Aviv, 1973), 1: 175-76. On page 347, note 8 gives as his source a verbal report to him.

57. *Kenesset Yisrael* by Reuben Zvi of Ostila (Warsaw, 1906), 7b-8a. See *Sefer Ha-Hakdamah ve-Ha-Petihah* by R. Gershom Hanokh Henekh of Radzyn, ed. Yeruham Latner (New York, 1950); this is the introduction of R. Gershom Hanokh to his father's *Bet Yaakov*. See pp. 28-40 for a defense of Rambam as kabbalist.

The Place of Ethics in Medieval Jewish Philosophy— The Case of Saadia Gaon
by
Menachem Kellner

This study examines the place of ethics as a distinct discipline in medieval Jewish philosophy, using as an example the case of Saadia Gaon. Before turning to the question itself, however, a considerable amount of preliminary discussion is necessary. This involves the definition of ethics as a philosophic discipline, as well as the question of the relation between ethics and religion in general and between ethics and Judaism in particular. This last, of course, raises the question of the relation between ethics and halakhah. In these areas I do not plan to settle any issues, only to raise them in order to explicate the problematic of Jewish ethics which forms the background against which medieval discussions must be seen.

Having described these matters it then makes sense to sketch in the historical background, touching briefly on the place of ethics in Bible and Talmud, the periodization of the discussion of ethics in Judaism, and, finally, the various approaches to ethics which we find in the medieval period. These matters will take up the first part of this essay. In the second part of this study I will examine the way in which ethics as a distinct discipline was dealt with by Saadia Gaon, the first of the medieval Jewish philosophers.

What, then, is ethics? The *Encyclopedia of Philosophy* distinguishes among three different but related uses of the term: "Ethics" may signify "(1) a general pattern or 'way of life,' (2) a set of rules of conduct or 'moral code,' and (3) inquiry *about* ways of life and rules of conduct."[1] The first two of these uses must be distinguished from the third. The first two relate to actual moral behavior, and it is customary to distinguish between two types of discussion concerning actual moral behavior: accounts of moral behavior (called "descriptive ethics") and prescriptive statements about how we ought actually to behave ("normative ethics"). The third use is more properly philosophical (or so, at least, it is taken to be by most academic philosophers) and seeks, not to make moral judgments, but to analyze them. This form of inquiry is often called "meta-ethics."

It will be noted that in the preceding paragraph I have distinguished different uses of the term "ethics" but have not yet answered the question posed at the beginning of the paragraph. "What, then, is ethics?" All I have done so far is to define "ethics" in terms of moral behavior or discussions concerning moral behavior. But what is moral behavior? Questions of ethics and morality are, in the first place, questions of value. Within the realm of evaluative issues the domain of ethics is determined by the particular values it seeks to describe, inculcate, or analyze. These values are generally conceded to be good and evil, right and wrong.

What sorts of things can be good and evil, right and wrong? One obvious candidate is works of art. After all, we often speak of good paintings and bad poetry. But there is the rub; "bad poetry," yes, but not "evil poetry." Evaluations of works of art, then, aesthetic judgments, are surely evaluations and share that characteristic with ethical evaluations but are withal distinct from them. This should further help to narrow down the domain of ethics. There seem to be two sorts of things which we evaluate when engaged in ethical (not meta-ethical) evaluation: human behavior and human character. Most ethicists relate the two (Kant is an important exception) and emphasize the former over the latter. Not all human behavior falls under the domain of ethics; if it did, psychologists, anthropologists, etc. would have to close up shop.[2] Rather, ethics deals with those aspects of human behavior which may properly be evaluated as right and wrong, good and evil.

Having come this far we immediately run into problems. The first of these has to do with ethics and religion. It seems intuitively obvious that the two must be related in important ways. Both seek to define what is good in human life and how one ought to structure one's life so as to maximize that good. Both are concerned with questions of ultimate value.

The problem was first raised, it seems, by Plato, in his dialogue *Euthyphro*. Do the gods love the good, he asked, because it is good, or is it good because the gods love it? In other words, does there exist some standard of morality independent of God's will (the good which the "gods" love) or do God's commands define morality (which is good, therefore, because the "gods" love it)? These alternatives appear to be exclusive and neither is particularly attractive. If God's commands define morality then, theoretically, were God to command us to torture young children it would be the morally correct thing to do.

Not to torture them would be the grossest immorality.[3] But this clearly offends our strongly held pre-philosophical notion that some things are inherently evil. Alternatively, if we assert that there exists some objective standard of good and evil by which even God's commands can be judged, then those commands are actually irrelevant to our moral evaluations, since the nature of right and wrong is theoretically discoverable without them. Even more important, were such the case, there could be no true obedience to God's commands as such: we would act in accordance with his commands not because they are his commands, but because they are right. Further, did such an independent standard of right and wrong exist, God himself would be obligated to obey it.

Historically, the relationship between morality and religion has gone through several stages. In the past, religion claimed to be the sole source of our knowledge of morality. Philosophy objected to this claim on the grounds that it made it impossible for people who did not accept revelation to be moral. Religion has generally responded to this objection with some variant of the doctrine of natural law, which claims that, at least in principle, all people can "read" God's moral demands from the very structure of the universe.[4]

Put this way, the question parallels the general problem of reason and revelation (or science and religion), which so dominated medieval thought. The answer usually presented for this problem—except by those who rejected either reason or revelation—was that at bottom reason and revelation taught the same thing. The question then naturally arises, if we have reason, why do we need revelation? A common answer (the one given by Saadia Gaon, for example[5]) was that revelation serves as a kind of short cut, graciously provided by God in his goodness, to the truths which reason could theoretically discover on its own, but only after a very long time and only with a great deal of difficulty, and without the satisfaction of being certain of having arrived at the truth.

This estimate of the relationship between morality and religion persisted until the 18th century. It was first challenged by Immanuel Kant. It was Kant's insight that in order to bind a person to obedience to a law, to obligate one to obey it, it had not only to be universally recognizable (the claim advanced against religion by philosophy, as noted above), but had to originate from within the person him- or herself. In order to bind us absolutely (or categorically, in Kant's terminology) a law cannot be hypothetical. Such a law only tells us how to achieve certain goals; it cannot obligate us to seek to achieve them. Indeed, the only thing that can obligate us to do anything is our acceptance of the obligation. The only law which binds unconditionally, then, is self-imposed ("autonomous") law.

Put in other words, Kant's claim is that obedience to commands as such, whatever their source, cannot count as moral behavior. Moral behavior must be free and unconditioned. The only behavior that satisfies this criterion is that which we freely take upon ourselves. Moral actions are distinguished from all others by the fact that they are prompted by no ulterior motives at all, but are done simply for the principle they embody.

Kant's critique of morality grounded in religion is radical and revolutionary. For, if a moral act must by definition be autonomous, then God and religion become irrelevant to morality. Morality and religion, despite their mutuality of interest, must be utterly divorced.[6]

Now, while no medieval thinker anticipated Kant and raised the issue of the autonomy or heteronomy of ethics, in those or similar terms, the issue was not entirely unknown to them, and it will be helpful to keep it in mind when we come to examine the place of ethics in medieval Jewish philosophy.

Another problem raised by the issue of Jewish ethics is the question of its scope. It is ordinarily assumed that ethical principles must both be consistent and apply universally. Normative ethical prescriptions must, then, apply across the board in every relevantly similar situation. But then what could *Jewish* ethics be? If we admit that the criterion of generality is fundamental to normative ethics, then the concept of a parochial normative ethic must be illegitimate. Put in simple terms, if something is right it is right and if it is wrong it is wrong. The notion of an act's being *Jewishly* moral or *Jewishly* immoral surely sounds odd.[7] This issue, too, was not explicitly discussed by medieval Jewish philosophers, but the way in which many of them couched their ethical discussions in general, as opposed to specifically Jewish, terms, as we shall see below, indicates that at some level they were aware of the problem.

Whereas the two issues just discussed involve problems in the relationship between any religion and ethics, there is yet a further problem which is unique to Judaism. This is the question of the relationship between ethics and halakhah. The problem arises because, while Judaism is not only a religion of law, it is preeminently concerned with it. This law, which is the central focus of Judaism (even if one wants to claim that such is not the case today, no one would deny that the claim is true of medieval Judaism) is not limited to religious law alone. While much of halakhah is indeed given over to religious or ritual law, it encompasses civil, criminal, and moral law as well. Since, then, halakhah contains an ethical component, we must ask whether it recognizes the existence of a Jewishly authentic ethical realm beyond itself. In other words, can there be *Jewish* ethical norms not included in halakhah?

It may be helpful to rephrase the problem in the following terms. As was stated above, ethics seeks to evaluate human behavior from the perspectives of right and wrong, good and evil. Every half-way literate Jew, however, knows that this is precisely a domain which the Torah arrogates to itself. The Torah seeks to teach us to do the right thing and seek the good and it further defines these terms for us. Another way of putting this is that Judaism is a *practically* oriented religion, seeking first and foremost to inculcate what it considers to be proper modes of behavior. The Torah, furthermore, takes as its fiefdom all of human life. That being so, what role, if any, can ethics play in Judaism?

This is a thorny problem.[8] If Judaism recognizes two authentically Jewish independent realms, one of halakhah and one of ethics, how do they inter-relate? Can halakhah be corrected on the basis of Jewish ethical considerations? Can ethics be corrected on the basis of halakhic considerations? In other words, if they are both authentically Jewish, is one still superior to the other? If not, what do we do when they conflict? If they never conflict, in what sense are they different?

There are further problems: if there exists a supra-halakhic Jewish ethic, what is its relationship to non-Jewish civil law? What is the obligation of the Jew with respect to imposing (either through force or education) that ethic upon non-Jews? Jews have traditionally argued that the halakhah applies to Jews only and have therefore not sought to enforce halakhic norms on non-Jews. But it is one thing for Jewish law to be parochial; the notion of a parochial ethic, as we saw above, raises real problems.

Yet further questions arise: if morality must be universally recognizable, then not only must Jewish ethics apply to all human beings, but it must be available to them as well. If a supra-halakhic Jewish ethic exists, is it really universally available and, if so, is there anything specifically *Jewish* about it?

As I said above, I have no intention of trying to solve these problems here. Raising them, however, points up the problematic of Jewish ethics in any period. It will serve as a useful background to our discussion below of the place of ethics in the medieval Jewish philosophic scheme, as exemplified by the thought of Saadia Gaon.

Although a number of recent writers have sought to argue that biblical Judaism is self-consciously aware, so to speak, of a distinct area of thought and action parallel to what we today call "ethics,"[9] it seems that the received opinion—that the Written Torah, while surely permeated throughout with what we would call ethical concern, does not see ethics as a separate department of human thought and action, distinct from other branches of Jewish law—is correct. To the extent that we may speak of Jewish ethics, then, the Written Torah is surely one of its two most important *sources*, while not itself a text which self-consciously teaches ethics.

The same situation obtains with the second major source of Jewish ethics: the corpus of rabbinic literature. Here too we have no separate, distinct text dealing with ethics in a self-conscious fashion (*Avot* not excepted), and no apparent realization that ethics is a department of thought which must be treated independently of other concerns. Rather, like the Written Torah, we have before us a group of texts which are permeated throughout with what we would today call ethical concerns.

It is only in the Middle Ages, and under the apparent influence of Greek categories of thought, mediated through Islam, that we find Jews composing works self-consciously and explicitly devoted to ethics. While the form adopted for these discussions might reflect Greek thought, the concern with right behavior is clearly not new. But we certainly find here, for the first time, a distinct Jewish ethical literature seeking systematically to expound upon morals and human conduct. Joseph Dan divides the ethical literature of this period into four categories: philosophic, rabbinic, pietistic, and kabbalistic. It is with the first of these that we are concerned here.[10]

The basic philosophic issue which underlay discussion of ethics among medieval Jewish philosophers had to do with the nature of God. The reason for that is relatively straightforward: the importance we attach to ethical behavior and the ethical goals we set for ourselves obviously depend upon our view of human nature. And since man is created in the image of God (according to Judaism) and finds his most perfect realization in imitating God (according to both Judaism and all medieval philosophy),[11] it follows that our estimation of man's nature depends to a great extent on our estimation of God's nature.[12]

Putting the matter rather broadly, if we follow Plato and define God as the Good, then we become God-like by making ourselves as good as possible. If we further follow Plato and view the soul as a separate entity which exists independently of the body before birth and can therefore survive the death of the body, we will be led to see the best form of human behavior as that appropriate to the soul in its pristine purity. Ethical behavior for Plato is that form of behavior which both makes us God-like and is appropriate to our souls. Such behavior, therefore, is our highest perfection.

If, on the other hand, we follow Aristotle and define God as thought, then we become God-like by thinking as much as possible in the best possible fashion. If we further follow Aristotle and view the soul as a power, force, or faculty which exists only potentially when we are born and can be actualized only through the process of intellection, we will be led to see the best form of human behavior as intellectual cognition, since only through such behavior do we actualize ourselves as human beings. Philosophy makes us human. On such a view ethical behavior is at best a propaedeutic to the truly human work of the intellect, but has no inherent value of its own. On this position the individual who returns to the cave after achieving intellectual perfection is destroying himself or herself as a human being. This view is essentially egotistical. It is also the view of God with which Maimonides thought he had to contend, and which informs the place of ethics *per se* in his philosophic system.

The first of the medieval Jewish philosophers to compose a treatise on ethics was Saadia Gaon.[13] Saadia's *Beliefs and Opinions* contains an entire treatise, the tenth and last, devoted to a systematic analysis of thirteen competing candidates for the *summum bonum*. He treats briefly of ethics, however, in an earlier treatise as well. This is the third treatise, "Concerning Command and Prohibition." It is here that Saadia introduces his famous distinction between rational and revealed commandments.[14]

In III.1 Saadia makes the following observation:

> I say, then, that logic demands that whoever does something good be compensated, either by means of a favor shown to him ... or by means of thanks.... This is one of the general demands of reason....

> Reason also demands that he that is wise does not permit himself to be treated with contempt or to be insulted.... Furthermore, reason demands that the creatures be prevented from wronging each other in all sorts of ways.... Reason also deems it proper for a wise man to give employment to an individual who performs a certain function and to pay him a wage for it, merely in order to confer a benefit upon him, since that is something that redounds to the benefit of the worker without hurting the employer.[15]

We have before us four requirements of reason. Now each and every one of these requirements of reason is something that we would ordinarily associate with ethics, not with rational science. After all, what are these four requirements of reason? The first is the obligation of gratitude, of repaying benevolent action in kind. The second relates to the respect due to the wise, and which a wise person will insist upon receiving. The third is the prohibition of harming others. The last class is not so much a requirement of reason as a propriety. It is what we may call supererogatory benevolence: being kind to others simply to benefit them.

It is obvious from this that Saadia was a remarkably decent and humane individual, since he saw these four qualities—gratitude, respect, avoidance of giving injury, and benevolence—as being required by reason and thus, to adopt another philosopher's idiom, as being clearly and distinctly true and not in need of proof. It is equally obvious, however, that his view of the requirements of reason differed from that of other philosophers, such as Aristotle before him and Maimonides after him. Both of these philosophers, and most others besides, restrict the realm of rational truth to the sciences, pre-eminently physics and metaphysics. What we have here, I would venture to say, is an indication of the essential Jewishness of Saadia's philosophizing. He, more clearly than his successors, sees the cash value of reason in proper behavior.

These four classes of requirements, Saadia informs us, "make up all the laws prescribed for us by the Lord" (p. 130). He divides them into two groups. The first group is made up of the first three requirements, while the second group consists of the last. Of the three classes of actions in the first group Saadia says, "Now the approval of each of these classes of acts that we have been commanded to carry out is implanted in our minds just as is the disapproval of each of the classes of acts that we are forbidden to commit" (p. 140). These, then, are what Saadia calls the "rational precepts of the Torah." The second group, consisting of the last class of requirements, "consists of things neither the approval nor the disapproval of which is decreed by reason, on account of their own character, but in regard to which our Lord has imposed upon us a profusion of commandments and prohibitions in order thereby to increase our reward and happiness" (p. 140). These are the so-called revelatory precepts.

Unlike the first group, these are commandments which we would not have been able to discover on the basis of our unaided reason, even though

> one cannot help noting ... that they have some partial uses as well as a certain slight justification from the point of view of reason, just as those belonging to the first general division have important uses and great justification from the point of view of reason [p. 141].

The distinction between the rational and revelatory precepts, then, turns out to be one of degree, not of quality. Both in the end turn out to be requirements of reason, the former more so than the latter. It may be impossible to be a little bit pregnant, but for Saadia it is, apparently, possible to be a little bit rational.

We have before us, then, four requirements which among them exhaust the practical teachings of the Torah (i.e., the commandments), acquiescence to which is demanded by reason, and all four of which are requirements of ethics as well as of reason. Oversimplifying a bit, we can summarize Saadia's position here with the following equation: Torah = ethics = reason.[16]

Saadia devotes the tenth and final treatise of *Beliefs and Opinions* to a discussion of "how it is most proper for man to conduct himself in this world" (p. 357). The title to this section immediately strikes the attentive reader—especially the reader who remembers that Saadia Gaon was first and foremost the Gaon of Sura and only secondarily a philosopher—as odd. After all, there can hardly be any doubt that for Saadia the most proper way for a man to conduct himself in this world is in accordance with the dictates of the Torah! And yet here he seems to be proposing an ethical system independent of the Torah. It will become clear below why this is not the case.

Saadia opens the treatise with the observation that since God is essentially one it follows by logical necessity that his creatures be composites. He bases himself here on an argument found in II. 1 (p. 96): "Since the creator of all bodies cannot be of the same species as his creatures, and since the bodies are many in number, it follows of necessity that he be one." That argument, of course, is for the unity of God. It can easily be turned around, as Saadia does here, and used as an argument for the composite character of God's creations.

Saadia uses the composite nature of human beings to argue against an approach to life which stresses one tendency or trait above all others. He writes:

> Now just as the material objects do not consist of just one of the four elements ... so, too, man's conduct in the course of his lifetime cannot logically be based on just a single trait. But just as in each instance the final product is the result of a combination of ingredients in larger

or smaller proportions, so, too, is man's behavior the resultant of a combination of his likes and dislikes in varying proportions [X. 1, p. 358].

It is Saadia's point in this treatise to argue that not only is human behavior in practice "the resultant of a combination of ... likes and dislikes" but that it *should* be such. His is an extended argument against monomaniacal devotion to one value or the development of one trait of disposition.

Human beings, then, must balance their competing traits, dispositions, desires, and impulses. What are these competing traits? Saadia lists and discusses thirteen "principal types of the [human] strivings" (X. 4, p. 364). These may be summarized as follows: (1) asceticism (2) eating (3) sexual intercourse (4) erotic love (5) wealth (6) children (7) building up the world (8) long life (9) dominion (10) revenge (11) wisdom (12) worship (13) rest. It is this discussion which makes up the bulk of Treatise X. Each of the thirteen strivings is described and support for its position as the highest good is found in Scripture. Each one of them is then subjected to criticism: "Each of these," Saadia says, "will be subjected ... to rational analysis" (p. 364). This rational analysis turns out to be an exposition of the ways in which one-sided devotion to any of the thirteen candidates for the *summum bonum* has deleterious effects on the devotee. In each case Saadia bolsters his argument with fairly extensive and—typical of this sensitive reader of the Bible—perfectly apposite citations from Scripture, countering the verses brought in support of each of the traits.

This last point helps us to understand what Saadia is doing here. He is examining various options for the highest good in life which Scripture itself can be interpreted as supporting. This discussion of "how it is most proper for man to conduct himself in this world" is necessitated by the fact that the Torah is open to misinterpretation on this point. This is, of course, a willful misinterpretation, dependent upon the wrenching of isolated verses out of context and reading them as if they existed in isolation from the rest of the Torah. It is to a correct reading of these verses and the exposition of the context in which they are read that Saadia devoted the tenth treatise of the *Beliefs and Opinions*.

Saadia's ethical treatise turns out to be an exaltation of a life of balance and integrated moderation, a life in which each natural human impulse is given its due (now greater, now lesser).[17] How do we achieve this life of balance, integration, and moderation? We can prove that no one good is the best of all goods; reason and common sense suffice for that, as Saadia showed in his detailed analysis of each *prima facie* good. But in order properly to balance these various competing goods we need wisdom. This wisdom may be achievable through reason in the long run but is presented in an accurate and accessible fashion in the Torah, the truest guide to "proper conduct in this world." This is the point of the nineteenth and last chapter of the tenth treatise, a chapter given over to a reading of several verses in Ecclesiastes. The upshot of Saadia's commentary here is that it is the wisdom of the Torah which guides us in actual, practical detail to the life of balance and moderation towards which we should all strive. Thus, there can be no ethic independent of the Torah. This parallels Saadia's claim, noted above, that without the Torah we would not know the details of the rational commandments.

The analysis of Saadia presented here supports and is supported by Eliezer Schweid's *"Torat Ha-Mussar Ha-Datit shel Rav Sa'adiah Gaon."*[18] Schweid argues in great and convincing detail that Saadia is concerned with presenting, not a theory of ethics, but a theory of *mitzvot*. Granted that this is what Saadia is doing, why does he argue that his theory of *mitzvot* is supported by reason? Saadia maintains that the Torah teaches certain theses about the nature of ideal human behavior. Among these are the claims that there is no one *summum bonum*, that the good life consists of a mixture of these putative goods, and that it takes wisdom of a certain sort to achieve the proper mixture. He also shows how the Torah rejects single-minded devotion to each of the proposed highest goods which he discusses. Why is he not content to leave his discussion at that without showing how each of these claims is supported by reason? It is because of his attempt to show the rationality of his (Torah-based) theory of human conduct that he is sometimes mistakenly interpreted as presenting a philosophical ethic, basically independent of Judaism and even of the rest of his book.[19]

The answer to this question relates to an issue brought up at the very beginning of *Beliefs and Opinions*, and allows further insight into the thematic unity of the whole book and puts to rest once and for all the theory that the tenth treatise is a kind of appendix tacked on to the book as an afterthought.[20] As is well-known, Saadia maintains that his primary purpose in composing the *Beliefs and Opinions* is to provide the religious believer with certainty that the doctrines accepted on the basis of received tradition are indubitably true.[21] He asserts that there are "three bases of truth and ... vouchers of certainty."[22] These are (a) knowledge gained by direct observation, (b) knowledge immediately and intuitively known as correct, and (c) knowledge inferred by logical necessity. To these generally accepted sources of certain knowledge, Saadia adds a fourth:

> As for ourselves, the community of monotheists, we hold these three sources of knowledge to be genuine. To them, however, we add a fourth source, which we have derived by means of the other three, and which has thus become for us a further principle. That is [to say, we believe in] the validity of authentic tradition, by reason of the fact that it is based upon the knowledge of the senses as well as that of reason,[23] as we shall explain in the third treatise of this book.[24]

Here we have for the first time in an authoritative Jewish text the beginnings of a statement on the relationship between reason and revelation, a problem which was to be central in the ensuing career of Jewish philosophy.

Much of Saadia's discussion in the introductory treatise of *Beliefs and Opinions* is given over to what might be called the habilitation of reason in the eyes of revelation. He argues that revelation itself "corroborates for us the validity of the first three sources of knowledge" (p. 18) and cites a series of verses from Scripture in support of this claim. He also refutes the idea that "speculation leads to unbelief and is conducive to heresy" (Introduction, 6, p. 26) on the grounds that "such an opinion is held only by the uneducated...." Saadia further argues (p. 27) that the prophets of Israel encouraged such speculation, and that the talmudic sages forbade it only when carried out incorrectly.

Indeed, Saadia does such a good job of proving the Jewish validity of philosophy that he finds himself faced with a different problem altogether: if reason is a valid and religiously appropriate method for arriving at certain truth on religious matters, what do we need revelation for? Saadia puts the matter in the following way:

> Inasmuch as all matters of religious belief, as imparted to us by our Master, can be attained by means of research and correct speculation, what was the reason that prompted [divine] wisdom to transmit them to us by way of prophecy and support them by means of visible proofs and miracles rather than intellectual demonstrations? [Introduction, 6, p. 31]

Saadia's answer to this question is that achieving truth on the basis of reason is a long, drawn-out affair, fraught with the possibility of error. If, therefore, God

> had referred us for our acquaintance with His religion to that art [speculation] alone, we would have remained without religious guidance whatever for a while, until the process of reasoning was completed by us so that we could make use of its conclusions. But many a one of us might never complete the process because of some flaw in his reasoning. Again, he might not succeed in making use of its conclusions because he is overcome by worry or overwhelmed by uncertainties that confuse and befuddle him. That is why God ... afforded us a quick relief from all these burdens by sending us His messengers through whom He transmitted messages to us, and by letting us see with our own eyes the signs and proofs supporting them

about which no doubt could prevail and which we could not possibly reject [p. 31].

Saadia's position may be expressed in the following analogy. Teachers' editions of high-school mathematics textbooks often are printed with answers in the back of the book to the problems set in the text itself. A person armed with such a key can work out the problems in the book and then check the answers arrived at against the solutions in the back of the book. Alternatively, one might not bother to work out the problems at all, relying altogether on the answers printed in the back of the book. Revelation is like an answer key to the problems of religion. We can work out the answers to these problems on the basis of rational speculation alone, checking them against the answers provided by the Torah ("the back of the book"), thus guaranteeing ourselves against error. Alternatively, we can avoid the trouble of working out the solutions ourselves and go directly to the answers provided by revelation. Revelation thus serves as either a corrective and guide to reason, guaranteeing that we use it properly, or as a shortcut, allowing us to arrive at certain truth without recourse to reason. Saadia, unlike Maimonides after him, sees both routes as valid. Philosophically inclined individuals, or those forced to defend Judaism against the attacks of others, will choose the first route, while individuals not so inclined or not so attacked will often choose the second route. Both routes lead to the same truth.

Returning to our discussion of Saadia's ethics we can immediately see the parallels. As we have seen above, ethical behavior depends upon the balance and integration of various goods. The wisdom necessary for achieving this balance is attainable by human beings—at least in theory—but the only sure way to achieve this wisdom is through the Torah. This is exactly parallel to the case of reason and revelation generally. Just as the Torah is a corrective and guide to reason, so is it a corrective and guide to ethics.

Relating Saadia to some of the general questions raised at the beginning of this essay, we may observe that in one sense Saadia can allow for the autonomy of ethics: since in the final analysis we can theoretically arrive at knowledge of the best life on the basis of reason alone, ethics can, again in theory, be independent of revelation. In practice, however, Saadia favored a heteronomous approach, basing our ethical decisions upon the wisdom of the Torah. It is probably safe to add that while one might, in theory, defer decisions on speculative matters till one has worked through the problems oneself, one cannot defer such decisions on practical matters. For Saadia, then, the Torah may be said to be much more immediately necessary for us in matters of ethics than in matters of metaphysics.

Similarly, with respect to the question of the uniqueness of Jewish ethics Saadia would argue that in principle, since ethics is, in the final analysis, rational, it is universal. Jewish ethics is individuated by its detailed prescriptions in the same way in which the rational commandments of the Torah are individuated by the detailed prescriptions of the *mitzvot*. Thus, we may say that there is a uniquely Jewish ethic in detail but not in general.

Since this uniquely Jewish ethic is taught in detail by the commandments of the Torah, and since in its general, rational principles it is equivalent to the teachings of the Torah, there can be no talk of a *Jewish* ethic independent of Jewish law.

Saadia leaves himself open in all of this to the possibility that someone will claim that since humans can arrive at knowledge of how to behave in general without the Torah, then God is essentially irrelevant to ethics. This is similar to the claim which could be raised against him that since humans can arrive at true knowledge of the universe without revelation, God and Torah are essentially irrelevant to our knowledge of the truths of the universe. Together these two points lead to the claim that God and Torah are essentially, in principle (if not often in practice), irrelevant to our perfection as human beings.

There can be no doubt that Saadia would have found these conclusions, especially as they are stated here, obnoxious. He would also, I submit, have found them ridiculous. True, he would say, we can indeed achieve true knowledge of ethics, physics, and metaphysics on the basis of our senses and reason without recourse to the Torah, at least in theory, and only with a very great deal of difficulty. But it is revelation, he would insist, that guarantees their truth! In effect, he separates two questions here. The first is whether or not truth and criteria of good and evil exist independently of God's will. The second is how we come to know these things with certitude. The latter, for Saadia, seems to be the more important of the two questions.

This solution is good enough for Saadia Gaon. But, unless he is willing to say that human reason itself cannot function independently of God (a point he may very well be happy to adopt), his position seems to leave him with ethics and metaphysics independent, in principle, of God and revelation. Whether or not this is indeed the case, however, must be the subject of a separate inquiry.

1. See *Encyclopedia of Philosophy* (New York, 1967), 3:81-82.

2. I do not mean to imply that these domains are not relevant to ethics; they certainly are.

3. See Maimonides, *Guide of the Perplexed*, III, 17, for the discussion of a Moslem sect (the Ash'ariyya) which to all intents and purposes upheld this view.

4. See Emil Fackenheim, "The Revealed Morality of Judaism and Modern Thought," in *Contemporary Jewish Ethics*, ed. M. Kellner (New York, 1978), 61-83. For an illuminating discussion of natural law and religious ethics see Steven S. Schwarzschild, "Do Noachites Have to Believe in Revelation?" *Jewish Quarterly Review* 52 (1962): 297-308 and 53 (1962): 30-65.

5. See below for a detailed exposition of this position.

6. For a valuable and very interesting discussion of these issues see Moshe Sokol, "The Autonomy of Reason, Revealed Morality, and Jewish Law," *Religious Studies* 22 (1987): 423-37.

7. For a detailed analysis of these issues see Menachem Kellner, "Reflections on the Impossibility of Jewish Ethics," *Annual of Bar Ilan University: Studies in Judaica and Humanities (Moshe Schwarcz Memorial Volume)* 22-23 (Ramat Gan, 1987): 45-52.

8. See Aaron Lichtenstein, "Does Jewish Tradition Recognize an Ethic Independent of Halakhah?" in Kellner, *Contemporary Jewish Ethics*, 102-23.

9. See, for example, Israel Efros, *Ancient Jewish Philosophy* (Detroit, 1964), and Shubert Spero, *Morality, Halakhah, and the Jewish Tradition* (New York, 1983), chap. 2.

10. See Joseph Dan, "Ethical Literature," *Encyclopedia Judaica* (Jerusalem, 1972), 6:922-932.

11. For studies of *imitatio Dei* in Judaism, see the articles by David Shapiro ("The Doctrine of the Image of God and *Imitatio Dei*," pp. 127-51) and Martin Buber ("Imitatio Dei," pp. 152-61) in Kellner, *Contemporary Jewish Ethics*.

12. I discuss this issue in my study, "Human Perfection in Maimonides."

13. Studies of Saadia's ethics include Nahum Arieli, "Tefisat ha-Mussar bi-Hashkifotehem shel Rasag ve-Rambam," *Da'at* 15 (1985): 37-66; Joseph Dan, *Sifrut ha-Mussar ve-ha-Derush* (Jerusalem, 1975), 16-21; Israel Efros, "Gishat ha-Sekhel el ha-Mussar lefi Rasag ve-ha-Rambam," *Tarbitz* 28 (1959): 325-29; Efros, "Sa'adia's General Ethical Theory and its Relation to Sufism," in *Seventy-fifth Anniversary Volume of the Jewish Quarterly Review*, ed. A. Neuman and S. Zeitlin (Philadelphia, 1967), 166-77; Efros, *Studies in Medieval Jewish Philosophy* (New York, 1974), 123-34 (this is identical with the previous article); Eliezer Goldman, "Torato ha-Etit shel Rabbenu Sa'adia Gaon," *Da'at* 2-3 (1978-79): 7-28; Lenn Evan Goodman, "Sa'adia's Ethical Pluralism," *Journal of the American Oriental Society* 100 (1980): 407-19; Goodman, "Sa'adia on the Human Condition," *Jewish Quarterly Review* 67 (1976): 23-29; M. Greenbaum, "Parashat ha-Middot ve-ha-Mussar be-'Emunot ve-De'ot' le-Rasag," *Darom* (Argentina), September-December, 1942 (I have not seen this study); M. Lazerson, "Al Torat ha-Mussar ve-ha-Mishpat shel Sa'adia Gaon," *Bitzaron* 6 (1942): 840-44; Henry Malter, *Sa'adia Gaon: His Life and Works* (Philadelphia, 1921), 247-60; Simon Rawidowicz, "Mishnat ha-Adam le-Rav Sa'adia Gaon," *Bitzaron* 7 (1947): 53-58 and 190-96; D. Rau, "Die Ethik R. Saadya's," *Monatsschrift fuer Geschichte und Wissenschaft des Judenthums* 55 (1911): 385-89, 513-30, and 713-28 and 56 (1912): 65-79 and 181-98 (I have not seen this study); Eliezer Schweid, "Emunah ve-Orah Hayyim shel Torah lefi R. Sa'adia Gaon," in *Yerushalayim: Pirkei Sifrut u-Vikoret*, Vol. 9-10, ed. Y. Eliraz and H. Kilai

Gaon," in *Yerushalayim: Pirkei Sifrut u-Vikoret*, Vol. 9-10, ed. Y. Eliraz and H. Kilai (Jerusalem, 1975), 135-51; Schweid, "Torat ha-Mussar ha-Datit shel Rasag," *Mehkarei Yerushalayim be-Mahshevet Yisrael* 1 (1982): 15-32; Isaiah Tishbi, *Mivhar Sifrut ha-Mussar* (Tel Aviv, 1970), 7-40; and Symcha Bunim Urbach, *Ammudei Ha-Mahshavah Ha-Yisraelit* (Jerusalem, 1971), 3:119-34.

14. For recent studies of this issue see Hannah Kasher, "Maimonides' Philosophical Division of the Laws" (in Hebrew), *Hebrew Union College Annual* 56 (1985): 1-7; Eliezer Goldman, (above, note 13); and Marvin Fox, "On the Rational Commandments in Sa'adia's Philosophy: A Re-Examination," in *Modern Jewish Ethics*, ed. M. Fox (Columbus, Ohio, 1975), 174-86, and the sources cited there in note 1. See also Josef Stern, "The Idea of a *Hoq* in Maimonides' Explanation of the Law," in *Maimonides and Philosophy*, ed. S. Pines and Y. Yovel (Dordrecht, 1986), 92-130.

15. I cite here (and below) from the translation of Samuel Rosenblatt, Sa'adia Gaon, *The Book of Beliefs and Opinions* (New Haven, 1948), 139. On Saadia's use of "reason" here, see the article by Eliezer Goldman cited in note 13 above.

16. This would not be Saadia's way of putting the issue. I certainly do not accept Julius Guttmann's claim that "it is especially in the realm of ethics that Saadia maintains the superiority of reason to revelation." See his *Philosophies of Judaism* (New York, 1973), 79. It is important to note here that for Saadia we need the Torah, even in the case of the rational commandments, since without it we could not know their details (III. 3, 145-47).

17. This should not be confused with Aristotle's doctrine of the mean. See Israel Efros's study in *JQR* (above, note 13).

18. See above, note 13. The position adumbrated here not only supports and is supported by Schweid, but expressly contradicts the interpretation of Saadia offered by Joseph Dan (above, note 13), 20-21.

19. See the sources cited by Goldman (above, note 13), 7.

20. See, for example, Isaac Husik, *A History of Medieval Jewish Philosophy* (New York, 1916), 46; Urbach (above, note 13), 119; and Colette Sirat, *A History of Jewish Philosophy in the Middle Ages* (Cambridge, 1985), 31.

21. On Saadia's purpose in composing the *Beliefs and Opinions* see the Introduction, chapters 2 and 6 (Rosenblatt, 9 and 27-28); Abraham Joshua Heschel, "The Quest for Certainty in Sa'adia's Philosophy," *Jewish Quarterly Review* 33 (1942-43): 265-313 and 34 (1943-44): 391-408; and Alexander Altmann, "Translator's Introduction" to *Saadya Gaon: Book of Doctrines and Beliefs* in *Three Jewish Philosophers* (New York, 1972), 20.

22. I. 1, p. 3.

23. These being the first and third bases of certain knowledge.

24. I. 5, p. 18.

Diplomatically Speaking: A Language Called "Ladino"
by
Nancy Kobrin

Theodor Herzl—we all know—was the father of modern Zionism. One of the most recent examiners of his life, the psychohistorian Peter Loewenberg, has recalled that—

> Herzl was born in Budapest in 1860—the second child of a highly assimilated Jewish middle-class family. His father was a bank director and timber merchant. Theodor was almost exclusively raised by his mother, his father being involved in business affairs and often away from home.... The Herzl home was noted for its formality and refinement, for attention to detail and externals.[1]

Emphasis in Herzl's home was placed upon how one should present oneself in public; there was recognition of a tension between the public and the private. His numerous biographers have noted that Herzl was a real "dresser," very well-mannered and exceedingly well-spoken. In short, he had all the "right stuff" for being a diplomat. Yet there is one particular aspect of Herzl's life story which has usually received less attention: the fact that his paternal grandfather,

Solomon Loeb Herzl, was an Orthodox Jew who originally resided in Semlin, Yugoslavia.

It is even less well known that Solomon Loeb Herzl was an ardent follower and financial supporter of the pious Sephardi rabbi Yehuda ben Solomon Hai Alkalai, his hometown rabbi. (Before I go any further, let me clarify my use of the term "Sephardi." Throughout this essay, I will attempt to restrict its meaning to those Jews who are descended from the forced emigres, the *megorashim* of Spain in 1492 and Portugal in 1497.) Rabbi Alkalai was born in Sarajevo in 1792 and died in 1878. He rose to prominence during the early 1840s as a charismatic, passionate preacher of a singular ideal—the ingathering of Jews to Palestine. Alkalai was among the earliest to write and disseminate this idea, and he did so in Ladino. His first book, a little known text called *Darkhei No'am*, published in 1839,[2] sets forth a radical interpretation of the talmudic text (*Sanhedrin* 97b) where the precondition for redemption is stated explicitly as *teshuvah* or repentance.[3] The hermeneutic involved plays out the literality of the root *shin-vav-bet* by linking *teshuvah* to *shivah*, the returning of Jews to Eretz Israel. Moreover, the obligation of *teshuvah* becomes an obligation of *shiva*, the physical, communal *aliyah*. *Teshuvah* then is a personal obligation as well as a communal one. In short, there was no theological excuse *not* to return to the Land.[4] Alkalai could thus handle the demands of piety, which had already stipulated the coming of the Messiah in order to initiate the ingathering, while his proposed doctrine technically went against the grain of the accepted pious norm of his time.[5]

Just as Herzl had been cognizant of his social environment, Alkalai was sensitive to the socio-political milieu of the Balkans, which was increasingly characterized by nationalistic struggles on the part of the *Volkerabfalle*,[6] the "bits and scraps" of the Balkan peoples, as Friedrich Engels dubbed them—all linguistically, ethnically and religiously different. It was a time of coming to grips with the concept of self-determination, and it was as if Alkalai came to internalize this extrinsic social reality and to realize that his neighbors' political agenda was not about to include legitimate geo-political space for the Jewish people in that particular region; so it was only natural to turn a little farther east, to Eretz Israel, in search of such space. And while we know that Alkalai traveled throughout Western Europe and had quite a following among many Ashkenazi leaders, to wit Herzl's grandfather, Alkalai nonetheless had the added responsibility as a *hakham*, a Sephardi rabbi, of providing leadership to his very own impoverished Ladino-speaking Jews of the Balkans. He therefore relied upon this communal language as his vehicle, and hence his choice of Ladino for *Darkhei No'am*. Even so, Alkalai also wrote many texts in Hebrew for the rabbinic intelligentsia.

I raise this intriguing aspect of Zionist history, little known to most people, precisely because the shared belief (or *creencia*, as Ortega y Gasset would have put it) which holds that Herzl came to the idea of a Jewish homeland on account of his having witnessed the anti-Semitism of the Dreyfus trial in Paris in 1894 remains common currency. It is such a widely embraced assumption that it has helped to overshadow a much more complex social matrix. Loewenberg is correct in asserting that "it is doubtful whether the young Herzl could have avoided hearing his grandfather talk of Alkalai and his dream of returning to the homeland." Furthermore, both Yehuda Alkalai's granddaughter and her husband David, who was also Yehuda's grandnephew, attended the First Zionist Congress in Basel in 1897. In Herzl's first Zionist novel, *Der Altneuland [The Old New Land]*, the character who heads the Land Acquisition Department is a Sephardi named Aladin. This character is said to have been modeled after Yehuda Alkalai's grandnephew David, who in fact was deeply involved in the reclamation of the land.[7] It is not my intention nor my task here to assess the exact impact, or to establish the source-influence effect, of Alkalai's teachings on Herzl's concept of a *Judenstaat*; however, what can be shown is that the received explanation of the origins of Herzl's Zionism has *tout court* eliminated the role of the Sephardim. As yet there is neither a critical edition nor an English translation of *Darkhei No'am*[8] and where Alkalai's writings have been included in the textbooks, he is presented and portrayed as a precursor, without an in-depth Sephardic frame of reference—simply placed alongside of Rabbi Zvi Hirsh Kalischer and Moses Hess in the usual concatenation.[9] This anecdote serves as a point of entry to a discussion of the rise and function of the Ladino language by moving it out from its usual peripheral position as that quaint, melodic, fifteenth-century Old Spanish of the *romancero* or ballad, popularized, romanticized and commercialized by some of today's best folk singers. Indeed, appreciation of the seriousness of this language increases when one considers its value as an untapped reservoir of Judaica.

Moreover, the case of Rabbi Alkalai's Ladino teachings being transmitted through Herzl's grandfather captures a moment, a slice of daily life of Jewry, where points of cultural exchange between Ashkenazim, Eastern European Jews, and Sephardim were constantly taking place. For it is at this elemental level where the process of identity-formation for any individual, Jew or non-Jew, takes place, and it is done through language, which allows for the construction of our social realities. This should signal that the study of all language in any form is of value. Yet oddly enough it is this level which is often overlooked and least understood.

The multifaceted nature of this process should also warn us of the inherent shortcomings of binary oppositions such as the one I have just deployed above—namely, "Ashkenazi" versus "Sephardi." In a text called *Mikhmanei Uziel*, written by the late Sephardi rabbi Benzion Hai Uziel (1880-1953), we find a folk explanation of how this opposition came into being. He wrote:

> The rabbis of Spain were powerful in opinion, and thought to annul customs which were not based on halakhic foundations. This contrasts with the rabbis of Ashkenaz, who strengthened custom and sought

support for it even if it seemed strange or without basis.... These opinions led the rabbis of France and Germany to have a negative opinion of the rabbis of Spain and their method. On the other hand, the awareness of independence and prominence [among Sephardi rabbis] leads one to find in many cases the mention of "Sefaradi" as an adjective of honor.... From this it followed that the Torah became like two Torahs and the people of Israel like two tribes, until a spirit from above will pour out over us and make us into one people.[10]

Such an opposition has helped to contribute to the solidification of the perception often expressed by the cliche that there exist only these two Israels, as if to say that there are no others. To think in this manner runs certain risks, such as being exclusionary and reductive. Take, for example, the way in which this old belief has been institutionalized with regard to the rabbinate in Israel, precisely along the lines of this dichotomy, with the Chief Ashkenazi Rabbi on the one hand and the Chief Sephardi Rabbi on the other, causing delicate difficulties as well as much pain (as in the case of Beta Israel, Ethiopian Jewry, who have never followed the Sephardi *minhag*, yet this is the rabbinic authority which mediates their communal concerns); nor is this to mention the complicated state of affairs for rabbis of the Conservative or Reform movements. Such a polarization between Ashkenazim and Sephardim also has the tendency to obscure the highly nuanced differences within each group. Under the rubric of Sephardi, one can easily demonstrate a tremendous heterogeneity from community to community, from the "oriental" Ladino of Smyrna to the western Ladino of Salonika, to say nothing of the full array of Sephardi communities in the New World, such as that on the Caribbean island of Curacao and the community in which I studied Ladino—Portland, Oregon. These differences have been retained and recorded by the specific, local use of language.

Proof of the widely varied world of Sephardica can even be found in the very number of names attributed to this so-called language, Ladino. As linguistic *res*, each signifier within its specific context signals a difference in function and usage. Many scholars have been plagued by this problem of name designation for Ladino, and have spent countless hours in debate over which name is the "correct" one. David Bunis has compiled a list of twenty-two terms for Ladino, and the list is still considered to be incomplete. Some of the terms are:

(e)spanyol(it), (e)spanyol ladino, franko (e)spanyol, franses, frenkish, "Giffoot," (leson) la'az (sefaradi), ladino, (l)ebran, leson sefaradim, levantino lingwa franka, portugal, romanse (espanyol), sefar(a)di, (lingwa) sefar(a)dit, "sephardita," "(lengua) vulgar," zargon, Spaniolic/-ish, and pseudo-scientific designations such as "Hebrew Spanish," "Jewish Spanish," "Jud(a)eo-Spanish," "Sephardic Spanish," etc.[11]

While the debate goes on, it has tended to shield the very issue of the proliferation in naming the object of inquiry. Each name carries insight into its mode of functioning. That Ladino can go by so many different aliases demonstrates its tenacity and dexterity in speaking and in evading a single, solidifying label, a label which would seek to halt a portion of its communicative movement. Yet from my title, the choice I have made is apparent. Why "Ladino"? The answer, while simple and anecdotal, should not be construed as uncritical. Before I began my formal studies in Ladino, I too had the tendency to use a variety of these cited terms, especially "Judezmo," which had been put forward by several scholars with the intention of creating for Sephardic Jewry a linguistic counterpart to the Ashkenazi language, Yiddish.[12] At the same time, the use of "Judezmo" would rectify the perceived gap between "Sephardi" and "Yiddish." Both terms, "Judezmo" and "Yiddish," would coalesce around the semantics of the idea of a Jewish language, since both retain the core of the word "Jew"—*judio, jidio* and *Yid* from their respective host medieval vernaculars of Spanish, Ladino and German. However, my habit of calling Ladino "Judezmo" changed on my very first day of formal studies, when I was resoundingly reprimanded by my teacher, who just happened to be a native speaker of the language as well as a gifted Hispanist and Romance philologist. He simply said, "Never say Judezmo; we call it 'Ladino.'" His authority made it anything but an uncritical call, and yet it pointed up the existing rupture in naming the language.

Yet the history of the origin of the term Ladino does not readily resolve this matter. To begin with, Jews were not the only people to have used the term Ladino to refer to a derivative of Latin; and therefore Judeo-Spanish Ladino should not be confused with the Ladino spoken by Italians of northern Italy, nor with the Ladino of the Romansch people of Switzerland.[13] According to the esteemed philologist of the Castilian language, Joan Corominas, "Ladino" derives from the term *Latinus* or *latino*, referring to Latin. During the Middle Ages, it was applied to Romance languages in opposition to Arabic, *la arabiga*, and to the Moors, who spoke in Arabic, at the end of the thirteenth century. It should also be pointed out that, from the later Morisco point of view, to write in Latin script was to write in *letra de kristyianos*—to use the Christians' alphabet. With reference to literary works, the term Ladino designated the more refined and cultured language close to Latin, principally during the fourteenth century. It is theorized that the adjective *ladino* developed from these two usages the meaning it has in Spanish parlance today, where it signifies *advertido, astuto, sagaz*, "sagacious, cunning, crafty."[14]

In Spain, as well as throughout most of Europe, knowing grammar meant knowing Latin. In fact, if one did not know Latin, one was called an *illiteratus*, that is, someone who did not know the Latin culture of the clergy, as opposed to the vernacular culture of the laity.[15] *Illiteratus* did not mean illiterate, as it does today. It is not until the writing of the *Gramatica sobre la lengua castellana*, by Antonio de Nebrija, that a grammarian would attempt to reduce a *modern* language to rules. Indeed, when Nebrija took his text to Isabel the Catholic, she understood its novelty but could not quite grasp its ultimate utility; whereupon Nebrija's companion, the Bishop of Avila, intervened and explained that since so many barbarian peoples and nations speaking foreign languages were being placed under the royal yoke, it was now time to think about the imposition of its laws upon the conquered peoples in the language of the newly consolidated Spanish state—in *castellano*, the imperial language.[16] Nebrija's book could not have been more timely. It is not without significance that four major events, all interrelated, took place during 1492, which is commonly referred to as the *annus mirabilis*, the year of wonder. They were: the publication of the first Spanish grammar, the discovery of the New World, the taking of Granada from the Moors—but for the Jews, the fourth event would record the year in their history as the *annus lutus*, the year of mourning, that is, the year of the Great Expulsion.

Thus, just as the date 1492 took on a radically different meaning for the Jewish community than it did for the Christian community, the term Ladino, from this latter perspective, also became recoded in a different direction to the canonically given entry by Corominas. Yet the tie which *ladino* retains is to the semantic register of high cultural texts, texts which originally derived from an association to the sacred language as opposed to those of popular culture. In its most restricted sense, and forming part of the debate over the name itself, "Ladino" initially is a term which is used to designate the literature of the "sacred" language of the Bible and the liturgy as translated into the Romance variant. Ladino comes into being some time during the thirteenth century, and at first refers to the reading of texts of high cultural status. Yet Moshe Lazar, in his entry in the *Encyclopedia Judaica* on Ladino, has asserted that to restrict the use of Ladino to this position of the semi-archaic is "hardly tenable" even though he cautions against assuming that there was at that time a full-fledged "Jewish language (as distinct from the dialects spoken in Spain)." We simply do not have the proof. This is not to say that the Jewish community on the Iberian peninsula had not already started to move toward coining its own specific brand of Old Spanish.

> There is no doubt that Jews interspersed their dialects with words or expressions borrowed from Hebrew (particularly terms and concepts connected with religion and ethics), and that they preserved archaic words and obsolescent forms longer than other people.[17]

However, it was only after the Expulsion of 1492 that Ladino began to be a specifically Jewish language. Although the Jews had been ejected from the Iberian Peninsula and thus cut off from its language while this was still in the process of evolving, they preserved the Spanish and Hispanic dialects that had been spoken and written before Cervantes and the Golden Age, and which basically reflected the phonetics, morphology, and syntax of the fourteenth and fifteenth centuries. As Lazar writes:

> A gap, wider or narrower according to the country to which the refugees fled, began to appear between the written and spoken language on the one hand and the language of secular and rabbinical literature on the other. The language of Bible translations and prayers, which remained more resistant to the words, expressions, and syntactic patterns of the local tongue, became, in the course of the centuries, less and less comprehensible to the masses.
>
> Distance from Spain, geographically even more than chronologically, was one of the most important factors in the increasing divergence between Ladino and Castilian Spanish. In the Amsterdam and London communities, for example, Jews continued to speak Castilian, which was constantly enriched by contact with the literature of the Iberian peninsula and the contribution of Marranos who returned to Judaism. In Italy, too, Castilian generally resisted tendencies to obsolescence and massive linguistic borrowings from languages such as Hebrew and Italian. On the other hand, in the communities of the Ottoman Empire, the language became more and more distorted under the pressure of Greek, Turkish, Arabic, and finally—when it was spread by the schools of the *Alliance Israelite Universelle*—French.... Leaving out of account the differences in phonetics and vocabulary between the so-called "Oriental Ladino" of Constantinople, Smyrna and Rhodes and the "Western Ladino" of Salonika, Bosnia, Serbia, Macedonia and Rumania, one finds that, between the 16th and 19th centuries, Ladino was a Hispanic language which had become petrified [like the Ladino of Rabbi Alkalai] on the threshold of the important changes pending in the Iberian Peninsula. It preserved all the characteristics of the language spoken and written in Spain when the grammarian Nebrija wrote his *Gramatica sobre la lengua castellana* (1492). Most of the linguistic characteristics of Ladino can be found in both Spanish and Latin-American dialects and patois—even as spoken today—and in medieval texts.[18]

In addition to this linguistic split between the communities speaking oriental and western Ladino, which together compose the eastern Sephardic communities, those Sephardic communities further to the west in Italy, Holland, Belgium, France, Germany (Hamburg), England and North Africa did not resort to Ladino. For after the expulsion they tended to follow the development of Castilian and Portuguese in the Peninsula, because of their proximity to it as well as extremely important financial trafficking with it. Such was also the linguistic practice for the Sephardic communities of the New World during colonization.

With the expulsion from Spain, the Sephardim took their daily language, a variant of medieval Spanish, with them to their new, dispersed havens. The break-up of that highly nuanced community of *Sepharad* had to juggle the impact of the above-described geographic diaspora. The language of this Old Spanish in transit would inevitably articulate that process of resettlement. Each community continues to generate its own particular dialect of Ladino, which reflects and constructs its own specific social reality. Ladino may be on the wane, but it is not dead.

Ladino is a Jewish language. The attributes of a judeo-language have often been summed up as the use of the Hebrew script and the retention of a high component of Hebrew and Aramaic. The fact that Ladino is written in Hebrew should not be surprising. During the medieval period it was common practice for Jews to write the vernacular of their host country in Hebrew script. For script graphically articulates the religious orientation of the community's sacred text; and yet the sonority of any Jewish language always resembles that of its host country's language. In Ladino's case it sounds like medieval Castilian Spanish. Hebrew script is literally its inscription of Jewish affiliation. What is of more importance is to understand the function of judeo-languages within not only Iberia but throughout the medieval world as a linguistic strategy or a strategic maneuver to maintain the ethos and ecology of the community. As the Jews were expelled from one country after another country, language—not only of the sacred text, the Torah, but language in all of its aspects—became increasingly more important because of the sense of shared experience and historicity. And wherever the Jews went, they moved toward coining their own particular brand of the host country's language.

In the case of medieval Iberia, the entire question of language was of particular importance because it allowed for Castilian to be elevated to a hegemonic national language, upon which the Spanish nation of Ferdinand and Isabel would be founded. Thus the aforementioned production of the first Spanish grammar by Antonio Nebrija was a linguistic strategy to consolidate and legitimate the existence of this new empire. Yet for those who were not in positions of power, what were their language options? Essentially there were three possibilities in theory and only two in practice. One possibility would be to endorse the same orientation as that of the nascent Spanish nation, which would entail the use of some Romance equivalent of Castilian Spanish. However, making the Romance more privileged than the Semitic would greatly complicate the sensitive issue of language and communal affiliation. It would have been like saying that Adonai spoke in Castilian, the language of the Christian community, rather than in the holy tongue. In theory the second orientation would be to resort to the language of the sacred Torah—Hebrew.

But the use of Hebrew had its own series of problems in acceptance, since the majority of the Jewish community no longer understood the sacred language of the Torah in its spoken form. The third possibility, the development of an authentic Sephardi response, would have to be articulated through the coining of a linguistic orientation which would permit a discrete, nonconfrontational way for the Sephardim to disengage the volatile problems of language, religion, ethnic identity and communial allegiance. They could do so by putting their own legends, poems, *romances* and translations of the Bible into Ladino, and by remodeling the vernacular of their host country through the recoding of the Romance language and the insertion into it of a heavy dose of critically important words, that is, valued expressions from the sacred Torah and from rabbinic literature. The retention of Hebrew and Aramaic, joined through the Hebrew script, would become the means for strengthening this special tie to Judaism and yet at the same time juggling the lived experience of pre-Expulsion Spain. This syncretism would not only allow the Sephardim to maintain their particular ethos and ecology, but, more importantly, it would allow them to assert their immediacy to Adonai and their validity from within their private culture, rather than be dependent upon the soon-to-be Spanish state, which, due to the policy of conversion of the Jews, was diametrically opposed to allowing the Sephardim space within the system. The process which was functioning behind the scenes, then, was that of creolization.

"Creole," a word which either calls to mind the realm of linguistics or that of New Orleans cuisine, is nonetheless an apt word precisely because of its ties to Spanish and Portuguese colonization. I use the term here in a broad, cultural sense as opposed to a strict, ahistorical, linguistic usage.[19] Creolization indicates the sense of intense intercultural penetration, recorded by this phenomenon of language mixing. The word first appears in fifteenth-century Portuguese as *criarse na colonias*, "to be raised in the colonies." The Portuguese term *criolo* enters Spanish in 1590 as *criollo*, meaning, "*Un blanco nacido en las colonias*" or "*un negro nacido en las colonias*" (a white or black born in the colonies).[20] While the word geographically points to the west and the New World, away from the trauma of Spain, the processes of creolization and syncretism were already being worked through in the peninsular languages, turning away momentarily from the centuries of intercultural penetration that lead to an age of intolerance, particularly with regard to race. *Criollo* articulates the action of the labelling of peoples through blood relations, that is, through an ideology related to *limpieza de sangre*, "purity of blood," which was diametrically opposed to the policy of conversion and which became the basis for the expulsion of the Jews. At the core of the policy of conversion was the desire to gloss over the diversity of people's origins. Upon converting, however, one soon found that the ideology had begun to show its cracks, since a distinction was then drawn between *cristianos nuevos* and *cristianos viejos* ("new" and "old" Christians).

With reference to Spain, one of the most intriguing aspects of the Sephardi sojourn was that, unlike any other country in Western Europe, it was the first pluralistic society, composed of Christians, Jews and Muslims. What these three major religious groups shared was not so much their theology (for there were major differences) but rather their special relationship to their respective scriptures—the Gospels, the Torah and the Koran. Each medieval community created special conditions of existence for their respective sacred books. And yet these communities had come into being precisely because they had been constituted by their holy books, which existed to be read and to be realized in their unique languages. The interpretation of the sacred text, be it the Torah, Gospels or Koran, always proceeded in a way which sought to insure the survival of the religious community. The coexistence of Christian, Jew and Moor has come to be called the Golden Age of oriental Spain—that picturesque utopian moment, characterized by the School of Translators in Toledo, who rendered classical Arabic and Hebrew manuscripts into Latin while the ordinary members of these communities quite naturally formed their own creoles in Spanish. And so it is that each religious community utilized its own script for Spanish. Spanish medieval texts are to be found not only in the Roman alphabet, as we predominantly know the language today, but also in the Hebrew and Arabic alphabets, with their respective borrowings, yielding a Christian variant of Old Spanish (which for facility I refer to as Castilian, though clearly we have instances of all its regional differences, oriented toward the kingdoms of Aragon, Cataluna, Galicia, etc.), an Islamic variant called Aljamia, and a Jewish variant called Ladino. Linguistically speaking, creolization is not a category of consciousness but rather a substantial everyday practice. Such texts as these identify that practice.

Their linguistic heterogeneity, which is substantiated by the various components of Romance and Semitic borrowings, also discloses that there was an abundance of meaning, and hence a panoply of possibilities for signification. There was no *aporia*, no loss or sense of helplessness in signifying. In addition, there was recognition of ethnicity by the fact that a speaker switched discourses. For to speak in Ladino was, according to the Judaic framework, to speak in a foreign language, a *la'az*, which is to say that the Sephardim themselves recognized that they were a Jewish people who chose to articulate themselves through the medium of a Romance language which was written in Hebrew script. Here, then, the naming of a discourse took up the issue of cutting across linguistic and cultural boundaries, as its hybridization sought a compromise through the retention of the respective sacred scripts and the sonority of the non-Semitic foreign majority, so that the Jews could give voice to their unique social reality.

The use of different scripts was a graphic marking of communal difference, of religious affiliation, whereby the process of identification to the sacred code could be reinforced. However, outwardly the sonority of these variants always sought to be consonant with the speaking practices of the majority, which by the time of the expulsion in 1492 meant a Catholic Spain. The Ladino text anchors the claim of ethnic sensibility, because a text retains the linguistic traces of cultural exchange. The interpenetration of these three major communities was constructed through the particular discourses which defined themselves one against the other. The competitive stance which this definition conferred on these groups was played out through the building of a homogeneous Spanish nation, devoid of Semitic peoples. The consolidating force of creating an empire involved suppression of those minorities which did not serve the hegemony of the state.

Thus, this linguistic paradise on earth was not to grow and flourish. Instead, the slow formation of Isabel and Ferdinand's Catholic Spanish nation—an undertaking which entailed major shifts of power, caused by the Reconquest, by resettlement of the frontiers, by colonization of the New World, by the demise of the feudal system and many other factors—led to the political act of literally emptying Spain of any minority which did not fit with the hegemony of the secular state. The Jews were expelled first, in 1492, and then a little over one hundred years later the Moriscos, or forcibly converted Moslems, were told to leave. The net effect of building a Catholic Spain on these languages resulted in the elevation of Castilian to the position of official state language and the suppression of Ladino and Aljamia. Ironically, once Castilian Spanish became the national language, it was deemed pure by the authorities, who were quick to overlook the fact that Castilian was the result of a pluralistic society. A similar case can also be made for French, Italian and Portuguese, which all got their starts as creoles. Creoles, then, are by their very nature the expression of cultural exchange before statehood is achieved and, hence, before a national language is imposed.[21]

Thus for as long as the Jewish community was able to live in the Iberian peninsula, Ladino was part and parcel of its survival tactics. In today's computer terms, Ladino can be thought of as a way of "hacking the system," that is, the method by which one manipulates the system in order to get it to work for one's own ends and without cost. Even after the Expulsion, the Jews continued to feel the need to preserve their specific language. Ladino became a way of remodeling symbols which allowed a speaker to retain a specific frame of reference oriented toward the private culture.

In the Ottoman East, from the fifteenth century on, there was to be a multitude of texts written in Ladino, ranging from Bible translations to prayer books to *Me'am Lo'ez*, the Sephardi commentary to the Bible, as well as dramas, poetry, novels, Alkalai's tract on Zionism and the beautiful and famous Ladino *romances*. It only stands to reason that there should be such a diversity of texts generated by this particular remnant of Israel. Yet culture is not simply a collection of books in which the collective memory is stored. More accurately, culture's principal task lies in organizing the world around us. Culture creates a sphere which makes social life possible.

As a final observation, a personal note regarding three perspectives on language from "the field" is in order. Several years ago, I had the good fortune to travel to three Sephardi communities which lie at various points throughout the Sephardi world. The first is Sarajevo, Yugoslavia; the second, Curacao; and the third, the *mellah* of Fez in Morocco. With regard to Sarajevo, I spoke with the *rosh ha-kal* (i.e., *kehila*) in my amalgamated academic medieval Spanish, Portuguese and Ladino (for I am not a native speaker). Nonetheless he understood me and was able to share with me his perceptions of the status of the community. There remain only 1,100 Sephardim in Sarajevo, the majority of whom are senior citizens. Almost all of the youth have made aliyah and now live in Israel; few speak Ladino. Since it was right before Passover, it was only natural to discuss wth him the famous Sarajevo Haggadah. When I returned home to Minnesota, I had planned a master class on Middle Eastern and Ladino music. For its preparation, the musicologist had left the lyrics of a Ladino ballad for my critique. It was *unheimlich*, that is to say, uncanny, that one of the ballads would be from Sarajevo. Its lyrics are:

Camini por altas torres	I walked among high towers,
Navegui por las fortunas	I sailed through storms
Onde gallo no cantava	Where no cock crowed
Ni menos me conocian	And where no one knew me.
Luvias caen de los cielo	Rain falls from the skies,
Lagrimas de los mis oxos.	Tears from my eyes.

And while I had read these verses many times before, I suddenly recalled them in a distinct way, immediately recognizing the *altas torres*, the tall towers of the ballad, as a reference to the more than 72 mosques which once adorned that flourishing Ottoman Empire town, in contrast to the tall posts of the modern chair lifts, a cultural imprint and residue of the 1984 Winter Olympics.

The second instance occurred while I was a scholar-in-residence at the oldest synagogue in the New World, and where I met with descendants of the first settlements of Jews to the New World, dating from 1651 and 1659—Curacao. Ladino has never been the spoken language of this community. However, today's inhabitants are very familiar with the idea of creole because of their island's own creole, a language called Papiamentu, which is basically a mixture of Portuguese and Dutch; and among the Jews of the community a bit of Hebrew sprinkled even with some Yiddish is to be heard. Yet it was the community's cemetery art that caught my ear, linguistically speaking. Its tombstones were imported from Amsterdam so that they could be engraved in Hebrew, but there are six other languages to be found on them as well—Portuguese, Spanish, English, Dutch, French and Yiddish, testifying to the diversity and longevity of the predominantly Sephardi community. As history would have it, the classic work on Curacaon Jewry was written by Isaac S. Emmanuel, their rabbi during the 1950s, who was a native Ladino speaker from Salonika. In his own words, Ladino served as an "inter-Sefardi medium of expression" within this community.[22]

My final observation from the field occurred in the Jewish quarter or *mellah* of Fez, Morocco. As in Curacao, Ladino was never the dominant language of the community. Nonetheless, as I walked its narrow streets I could not help thinking of Canetti's voices from the *mellah* of Marrakesh, and recalling too his special tie to his mother's tongue, which was Ladino. This master of German prose, a recipient of the Nobel Prize for Literature, named his memoirs *Die gerettete Zunge [The Tongue Set Free]*. In them he wrote of his drivenness as a person fascinated by language:

> Part of it, certainly, was a greater liveliness, the *swiftness of Ladino* [my emphasis], which I had spoken as a child and which had remained, as a peculiar tempo, in the slower languages like German and even English.[23]

The need to attribute this language experience to Ladino serves us as a window onto the lived experience of a Sephardi's view of his or her world. This seems to me to demonstrate a strategic maneuver, a certain diplomacy of speech—from which I take my title. "Diplomatically speaking," then, is the ability to see one's own language through the existence of other people's languages. The Ladino, be it of a Sarajevan ballad, Yehuda ben Alkalai's tract on Zionism or Elie Canetti's childhood memories, surely enunciates such a practice.

1. Peter Loewenberg, *Decoding the Past: The Psychohistorical Approach* (New York, 1982), 103.

2. For his complete works see *Kitve ha-Rav Alkalai* (in Hebrew), ed. Yitzhak Rafael (Jerusalem, 1974), 2 vols. The actual title of his first Ladino-Hebrew text is taken from Prov. 3:17: "Her ways are ways of pleasantness and all her paths are peace " (*The Holy Scriptures* [Jerusalem, 1969]), wherein *darkhei no'am* refers to the "delightfulness of God," according to Brown, Driver and Briggs, *English Lexicon of the Old Testament* (Oxford, 1907, 1977).

3. *Encyclopedia Judaica*, s.v. "Alkalai, Judah ben Solomon Hai."

4. The talmudic passage in question is grounded in a verse taken from Jer. 4:1: "If thou wilt return, O Yisra'el, says the Lord, return to me: and if thou wilt put away thy abominations out of my sight, without wavering, and wilt swear."

5. Halpern writes: "... leading theorists among the religious proto-Zionists, such as the rabbis Judah Alcalay and Zvi Hirsch Kalischer, had very actively advocated the interpretation that the resettlement of Palestine, the cultivation of its soil in accordance with Biblical laws, and even the rebuilding of the Temple were initial, preparatory stages of the Messianic times." Ben Halpern, *The Idea of the Jewish State* (Cambridge, Mass., 1961), 87. His source is *Rabbi Yehuda Alkalai-Rabbi Tzvi Hirsh Kalisher, Mivhar Kitveihem* (1945), 43ff., 127ff.

6. Istvan Deak, "A Conglomerate Country," *The New York Review of Books*, 7 November 1985.

7. *Encyclopedia Judaica*, s.v. "Alkalai, David." It should be added that there is a certain irony in all of this, in that Rabbi Yehuda Alkalai was a bit of a character himself and, like his grandnephew, was written into a novel—by Yehuda Burla, *Ba-Ofek* (On the Horizon), 1943.

8. Only one of Yehuda Alkalai's texts, *Mevasser Tov*, has been translated into English; it appeared in London in 1856 under the title *Good Tidings*. Its title page appears in the *Encyclopedia Judaica* under the entry for Judah Alkalai, op. cit.

9. See, for example, Arthur Hertzberg, *The Zionist Idea: A Historical Analysis and Reader* (Westport, Conn., 1959).

10. See the *Bulletin* of Congregation Shearith Israel, New York City, No. 2 (Heshvan-Kislev, 5746/November, 1985). It is interesting to note that these remarks were translated and excerpted for an announcement that the synagogue would host a series of lectures on this very dichotomy of Ashkenazim versus Sephardim, with the stated objective of overcoming differences.

11. David Bunis, "Problems in Judezmo Linguistics," *Working Papers in Sephardic and Oriental Jewish Studies* 4 (May, 1975).

12. For a full accounting of the term "Judezmo," see David L. Gold, "Dzhudezmo," *Language Science* (October, 1977), 14-16. He argues against the claim that "Judezmo" is just a recent calque of "Yiddish" by maintaining that its occurrence has been recorded by field work. Yet "Ladino" also occurs in the field, and its occurrence signals that it performs a certain function that has yet to be determined. There are, to the best of my knowledge, no statistics on the rate of frequency of these terms, which would not necessarily legitimate or validate their exclusive usage anyway. In his closing argument his proposal is clear: "In the Dzhudezmo-speaking community, unfortunately, there have been no native linguists or large-scale Dzhudezmist movements to popularize the native taxonomy in research circles, and this task has therefore fallen to others [i.e., non-Sephardim]. Granted, however, that *Dzhudezmo* is still infrequent outside the native

community, one may nonetheless hope that sometime and somewhere people will begin using it. This terminological modification should be no harder to make than others on record." Yet the fact remains that "Ladino" still exists and persists quite strongly outside this circle of desired reform.

13. See Tristiano Bolelli, "La lingua che parliamo—difesa del Ladino: L'antica civilita delle Dolomiti," *La Stampa*, 20 August 1985, 3.

14. Joan Corominas, *Breve Diccionario Etimologico de la Lengua Castellana* (Madrid, 1973), 351.

15. David Hall, "Introduction," in *Understanding Popular Culture: Europe from the Middle Ages to the Nineteenth Century*, ed. Steven L. Kaplan (New York, 1985), 8.

16. The original text is: "El tercero provecho deste mi trabajo puede ser aquel que, cuando en Salamanca di la muestra de aquesta obra a vuestra real Majestad, me pregunto que para que podia aprovechar, el mui reverendo padre Obispo de Avila me arrevato la respueta; respondiendo por mi, dixo que despues que vuestra Alteza metiesse debaxo de su iugo muchos pueblos barbaros naciones de peregrinas lenguas, y con el vencimiento aquellos ternian necessidad de recebir las leies quel vencedor pone al vencido, con ellas nuestra lengua, entonces, por esta mi *Arte*, podrian venir en el conocimiento della, como agroa nos otros deprendemos el arte de la gramatica latina para deprender el latin." Antonio de Nebrija, *Gramatica sobre la lengua castellana*, ed. Antonio Quilis (Madrid, 1980), 101-102.

17. *Encyclopedia Judaica*, s.v. "Ladino."

18. Ibid.

19. Nonetheless, a good text on this subject, with specific reference to Papiamentu, the creole of Curacao, is R. B. LePage and Andree Tabouret-Keller, *Acts of Identity: Creole-based Approaches to Language and Ethnicity* (New York, 1985).

20. Joan Corominas, "Criollo," *El Dicionario Etimologico de la Lengua Castellana*, 178.

21. These comments are a recapitulation of an in-depth argument set forth in my doctoral dissertation on the question of language during the late medieval period in Spain. See Nancy Kobrin, *Moses on the Margin: A Semiotic Analysis of Eight Aljamiado Legends on the Pre-Islamic Figure of Musa* (Ph.D. diss., University of Minnesota, 1984), chap. 4.

22. Isaac S. Emmanuel, *Precious Stones of the Jews of Curacao: Curacaon Jewry 1656-1957* (New York, 1957), 111.

23. Elias Canetti, *The Tongue Set Free: Remembrance of a European Childhood* (New York, 1979), 205. In the German original the term Ladino is not used by Canetti to refer to the private family language:

Was aber soll man von diesem Eifer des Sichervortuns denken? Sicher spielte eine größere Lebhaftigkeit dabei mit, das Rasche des Spanischen, das ich als Kind gesprochen hatte und das mir als etwas absonderliches Tempo auch in den langsameren Sprachen wie dem Deutschen oder gar dem Englischen geblieben war.

Elias Canetti, *Die gerettete Zunge: Geschichte einer Jugend* (Munich, 1977), 285. In an earlier passage of his memoirs, Canetti refers to Ladino as *altertumliches Spanisch*, translated as "an ancient Spanish." See respectively the German original, 18, and the English translation, 10.

Nahmanides' *Commentary on the Torah*
by
David Novak

There is a raging debate among educators as to what makes a book "great" enough to be required reading in the liberal arts curricula of leading American colleges and universities. The debate is much more than academic in any usual sense. It is concerned with the very political issues of values and authority. Since most of the persons who will have power and influence in the foreseeable future are now being educated in these leading colleges and universities, and since what they are now studying will surely influence their future thought and action, the choice of what they are to be now studying (and, by inference, not studying) is a political judgment about what values are to be primary and by whose authority they are to be implemented. Thus, political and cultural radicals of various persuasions charge that what has heretofore constituted the Great Books canon has been based on a bias towards the values and authority of white, European males and a prejudice against non-whites and females. Political and cultural conservatives, most prominently represented by Allan Bloom, have defended the Great Books canon as being based on what is most rationally impressive in the history of our civilization.[1]

The debate as it now stands is undecidable precisely because any true canon is based upon *one* primary text upon which all subsequent texts selected for the canon are essentially commentaries, in a broad sense. For defenders of the old Great Books canon, like Allan Bloom, that one primary text would probably be Plato's works, especially his masterwork, the *Republic*. (Indeed, Bloom has published his own translation of and commentary on this seminal work.[2]) However, even a work as venerable as the *Republic* is not one which plays any definite role in the life of our culture. There is nothing in our law or custom which affords the *Republic* the role of being publicly read as sacred writ, something which everyone is to regularly hear together. Hence, without an undisputed primary text, all talk of "canon" in any normative context has no criterion of judgment to which differing views can appeal. It would seem, then, that canon only has a political justification when there is a text which a society accepts as revealed, that is, coming from a source which transcends all the power interests in that society, and to which all the members of that society must look for their basic norms.

When it comes to canon, that is, to deciding what constitutes a "great" book, we Jews are in a much happier position than the academics who are debating about the politics of college and university curricula. We do have *one* primary text, and that text is the Torah. It itself is not *a* great Jewish book; rather, it is the criterion whereby all other Jewish books are judged to be great or not. Its greatness, for Jews, is because it is God's primary revelation to his people, a revelation which can only be elaborated, but never diminished, by any subsequent revelation or interpretation. A Jewish book is "great," therefore, only if it is a good commentary on the Torah. Indeed, Judaism itself, by its institution of public reading of the Torah in the synagogue, has made the Torah the prime political document for Jews.[3] (And I have never heard of any synagogue, irrespective of the especially vast theological and liturgical differences between synagogues today, where the Torah is not regularly read in one way or another.)

The Content and the Context of the Torah

Jewish commentary on the Torah is concerned with two levels of meaning: *peshat* and *derash*. The distinction between these two levels of meaning can best be understood if we can see the relation between content and context in any text.

If a text is primarily descriptive, that is, if its purpose is to present the reader with information rather than instruction, then content and context are closely related *within* the text itself. In fact, they are more often than not indistinguishable. The meaning of this kind of text is very much self-limited by its own time and place, which are of course separate from every reader except those who are most contemporary with it. When the Torah is read this way, the type of meaning which emerges is *peshat*, namely, "ostensive" meaning. Although this *peshat*-type reading of the Torah text characterizes most modern "critical" textual scholarship, it is not antithetical to the Jewish relationship with the Torah text as long as it is not the primary way of reading the Torah text by Jews.[4]

Scripture's ostensive meaning was exclusively affirmed only when the rabbis could not derive any immediately normative meaning from the text for their own contemporaries.[5] But when they could, and that was the case more often than not, the rabbis did not allow *peshat* meanings to distance the reader (or, better, the *hearer*) from the normative thrust of the text.[6] They did not allow the text to be enclosed within its own internal context or within the context of the time and place of its writing. Whenever they could, they engaged in *derash*, namely, searching the text for its meaning here and now. In order to accomplish this, the context of the text had to be seen not within the text itself, written as it was in another time and place, but rather within the life of the people as they were living here and now. The assumption is, of course, that there is ultimately no gap between the life of the Jewish people and the text of the Torah.[7]

From this it follows that all great Jewish books—books justifiably great by these internal Jewish criteria—are *derash* in one form or another, that is, they are essentially Torah commentaries, whether arranged according to the order of the Torah text or not. Furthermore, it follows that any such "commentary" is *great* if it is not basically limited to the concerns of one generation of Jews, but addresses itself to the issues with which Jews *qua* Jews must be concerned in every generation. By this criterion, Nahmanides' *Commentary on the Torah* is, without a doubt, a great Jewish book.

The Reasons for the Commandments

The very need for the text of the Torah to be as normative as possible is the main incentive for *derash*, both for discovery of the more precise norms governing action (halakhah) and the less precise norms guiding thought (aggadah). Inevitably, the search for these elaborated norms involves the search for the underlying purposes of the Torah, especially the *ta'amei ha-mitzvot*, the "reasons for the commandments." For if the commandments are to be expanded, then that orderly expansion requires some surmisal of the direction that the divine Lawgiver intended for His Torah.[8] Indeed, the search for the reasons for the commandments can be seen as the objective correlate of the subjective requirement that the one performing a commandment do so with proper intention (*kavvanah*). Now *kavvanah* is basically of two types. The first type is the intention that one is performing an act as a divine commandment in general (*kavvanah le-mitzvah*).[9] Thus, the formula of the benediction required for the performance of most positive commandments is the same, namely, that God "sanctifies us with His commandments and commands us" to do such-and-such. Here what is intended is the will of God, irrespective of what it is that we are being commanded to do by the specific commandment. However, there is a second, deeper type of *kavvanah*. It is the intention of the end of the specific commandment, namely, how one comes closer to God by performing this specific act. It is usually called "the intention of the heart" (*kavvanat ha-leb*).[10] What is intended here is the wisdom of God. When the phenomenology of this deeper *kavvanah* is seen, it is clear that it is the subjective motivation for searching for the reasons of the commandments, a motivation more genuinely religious than mere intellectual curiosity.

For Nahmanides, it is the proper intention of the heart that distinguishes authentic religious action from what Abraham Joshua Heschel called "religious behaviorism."[11] Thus when questioning why the Torah had to give a general commandment "you shall be holy" (Lev. 19:2), inasmuch as all the specific commandments are designed to make us holy, Nahmanides presents the striking phrase that one can "be loathsome within the strict limits of the Law" (*nabal bi-rshut ha-Torah*).[12] In other words, the observance of the legalities of the Torah does not insure one of becoming the holy person, which is the Torah's ultimate intention. Nahmanides, of course, is not arguing that holiness can be achieved apart from the observance of the specifics of the Torah, and certainly not contrary to them (as, for example, Martin Buber would later argue).[13] For him, these specifics are necessary but not sufficient for the true fulfillment the Torah intends.[14] Surely the requirement of *kavvanah* makes this clear even at the level of practical observance, let alone at the level of actual contemplation.

The rationalist Jewish theology of the Middle Ages, especially that theology influenced by Aristotelian teleology (namely, the assumption that there are always purposes in nature and human action), provided a stimulus and a method for the search for the reasons for the commandments. Thus Maimonides, the most important theologian influenced by this philosophy, saw all of the commandments as being for the sake of either the improvement of the body and society (*tiqqun ha-guf*) or the improvement of the soul (*tiqqun ha-nefesh*).[15] In the third section of his theological masterwork, the *Guide of the Perplexed*, he tried to show how the reason for each of the specific commandments could be discerned by using this general rubric.

As impressive as this method of inquiry might be intellectually, it entails some religious dangers. Take, for example, the reason Maimonides gives for the prohibition of eating pork. In the *Guide*, he emphasizes how the filthy conditions under which pigs live make pork an unhealthy food for the body.[16] However, this reason can also be used to avoid the prohibition if one can show that it is possible to raise pigs under hygienic conditions. In other words, if the prohibition has such a general reason, it is possible to fulfill the reason by means other than the specific prohibition of eating pork. The same religious problem arises when one sees the reason for a commandment being the improvement of the soul. If, for example, the purpose of the commandment to study the Torah is to apprehend metaphysical truths, and if these truths are capable of being apprehended (at least in principle) by all persons possessing moral and intellectual excellence, then does not general metaphysics ultimately displace the study of the Torah as the highest human activity?[17]

Even though Maimonides most definitely emphasized the authority of the commandments of the Torah irrespective of their reasons, religious concerns about the actual antinomian use this approach might (and, probably, did) lend itself to led the rabbis of northern France to actually ban the study of Maimonides' theological works. The controversy over Maimonides and the ban on his theological works, the so-called "Maimonidean controversy," came to a head in 1232. The Jewish world seemed to be polarized between pro- and anti-Maimonideans. A compromise was attempted, however, by a thirty-eight-year-old Spanish rabbi, Moses ben Nahman Gerondi (Nahmanides), already an important halakhic authority enjoying respect from all quarters of the Jewish world. Although himself concerned about the dangers entailed by a philosophical approach to the Torah and its commandments, Nahmanides defended Maimonides by indicating that the latter's rationalist theology was not meant for the masses of faithful Jews, but that it was only meant for those who had been exposed to philosophy and who, therefore, required philosophical justifications of Judaism for their own religious stability.[18] But Nahmanides' defense of Maimonides indicated that he too believed that there were indeed reasons for all the commandments of the Torah.[19] Where he differed from Maimonides, and from all the rationalist Jewish theologians both before him and after him, was in his insistence that the reasons for the commandments were not grounded in general metaphysics, but rather in uniquely Jewish theological ideas. One sees this project of his in all of his writings, but it became the true leitmotif of his masterwork, his *Commentary on the Torah*, a work he began in Spain before his expulsion in 1267, and which he completed shortly before his death in the Land of Israel in 1270. And, as any careful study of Nahmanides' work shows—certainly a careful study of his *Commentary on the Torah*—his agreements with and his differences from Maimonides comprised a major portion of his thought.

Commandments Based on Nature and Reason

It has been the tendency of some scholars to assume that because Nahmanides was so opposed to Greek metaphysics, especially the metaphysics of Aristotle, he rejected the idea of a natural order.[20] Since the rejection of nature also entails the rejection of any general type of reason adequate to understand this natural order, it seems to follow that Nahmanides was an "anti-rationalist." However, for Nahmanides, the rejection of Aristotelian metaphysics does not entail the rejection of natural order and its correlate, general reason. Quite the contrary, by affirming the reality of both, without metaphysical underpinning, Nahmanides is actually able to be more of a rationalist than Maimonides, especially when dealing with commandments governing social relations (*bein adam le-habero*). This can be seen when we compare Maimonides' treatment of the seven Noahide laws with that of Nahmanides.

The seven Noahide laws are those laws which the rabbis asserted were binding on all humankind (who are the "sons of Noah").[21] Since these laws contain prohibitions of such things as murder, incest and robbery, which are by no means unique to the Jewish people, there have been many Jewish theologians who have taken them to be evident to all rational persons and, therefore, binding on them as rational commandments (*mitzvot sikhliyot*).[22] They are what later Jewish theologians (following Stoic and Christian philosophers) called "natural law."

In a famous passage in his *Mishneh Torah*, Maimonides stated that anyone who accepts these laws only because of rational inclination (*hekhre ha-da'at*) is not considered worthy of the bliss of the World-to-Come, something which "the pious of the nations of the world" are assured.[23] Furthermore, in a passage in his earlier *Commentary on the Mishnah*, Maimonides rejects the whole concept of "rational commandments."[24] Despite the fact that some scholars have seen in these two passages a rejection by Maimonides of any rational natural law morality, I have argued elsewhere that Maimonides was, in fact, only rejecting a natural law morality not adequately grounded in a true metaphysical constitution of nature and reason.[25] In other words, Maimonides was rejecting any immediately evident moral norms as having any religious validity, however prudent they might actually be, unless their metaphysical status was affirmed.

Nahmanides, on the other hand, did not see that the foundation of morality required metaphysics. For him, morality had to be ultimately included in specific revelation from God, but since that revelation is historical, it does not function as any kind of rational presupposition for morality. One does not, indeed cannot, simply follow reason from practical to intellectual excellence. One does not come to revelation, therefore, but rather revelation can only come to one when God so wills it. As such, whatever morality one can learn for oneself is much more direct for Nahmanides than it is for Maimonides. This comes out in a number of comments by Nahmanides, but in contradistinction to Maimonides' view of the status of the Noahide laws, the following is most illustrative of his position.

> Violence is robbery and oppression ... for violence is a sin which is known and publicly accepted (*ve-ha-mefursam*) ... and the reason is because it is a rational commandment (*mitzvah muskelet*), for which there is no need for a prophet to give a [divinely revealed] commandment.[26]

It seems as though Nahmanides regards universally accepted morality as being a precondition for revelation. Thus, in writing about the patriarchs, with whom the Torah is very much concerned before the Sinaitic revelation, Nahmanides points out:

> And so you find that the patriarchs and the prophets conducted themselves in a universally accepted manner (*derekh eretz*) ... and it is a matter of inference *a fortiori*, namely, just as the patriarchs and the prophets who went to do God's will conducted themselves in a universally accepted way, how much more so should ordinary people [do so]![27]

Commandments Based on History

In dealing with those commandments whose reasons are immediately evident, Nahmanides is basically dealing with those commandments which are called *mishpatim*, namely, "judgments" between human beings in the ordinary affairs of society. However, he makes it quite clear, as we have already seen, that the realm of nature (including human political nature) is not the realm where the true relationship between God and humans is to be located. For nature implies a continual order, one which does not admit any innovation. However, the most elementary fact about God that humans are to recognize is that God is Creator, that the universe is the result of his totally free will and that God can intervene in the affairs of his universe at any time irrespective of the order of nature. Nature's order is only *usual*, but it itself has no inherent necessity. This is why the Torah places such stress on miracles, for it is through miracles, especially miracles of a spectacular kind (*nissim mefursamim*), that God demonstrates his creative power over the universe he created.[28]

The problem with this assertion is the fact that these spectacular miracles were performed centuries ago, and even then they were performed rarely. What connection does the ordinary Jew have with these great events so that he or she too can experience them and thereby appreciate God's creative power and providence? Nahmanides sees the Torah's solution to this very real religious problem in the function of those commandments called *edot*, "testimonies," namely, those commandments based on history. Thus when dealing with the Torah's commandment that the Exodus "be a sign upon your hand and a symbol between your eyes, for with a strong hand the Lord brought us out of Egypt" (Exod. 13:16), which rabbinic tradition saw as mandating the regular wearing of *tefillin*, Nahmanides, in one of his longest comments, wrote:

> This is because God does not perform a sign (*ot*) and a demonstration (*mofet*) in every generation to be seen by every evildoer and denier (*kofer*). So he commands us that we should continually perform a memorial (*zikaron*) and a sign of what our eyes saw.[29]

In this comment, whose main points he repeated on many other occasions, Nahmanides emphasizes what might be called a participatory view of history. We moderns, on the other hand, usually have what might be called an illustrative view of history.

For most moderns, the method for looking at history has become defined by the social sciences. The social sciences, modelling themselves on the natural sciences, attempt to discover regular patterns of human behavior. There is a concerted attempt to see all events as examples of repeated processes within the overall human condition. History becomes, then, the gathering of data from the past, data which broadens the number of examples to illustrate any process which is of contemporary interest. Here the interest in the past is determined by the interests of the present and its projections into the future. In sum, then, all historical events are ultimately reduced to the more basic processes they illustrate.[30]

Nahmanides' view of history, conversely, reflects a much more ancient assumption, namely, that human life in the present, including all the normal processes of human behavior, derives its true meaning from great events in the past. As such, the task of human thought and action is not to incorporate the events of the past into the processes of the present, but rather to see the processes of the present as symbols of these great past events.[31] For Jews, these regular processes are precisely those commandments whose obvious function is to enable persons in the present to participate symbolically in these great (and rare) past events.

By emphasizing the active nature of this symbolic participation in the great events of the past, when God made himself so powerfully manifest to the people of Israel, Nahmanides indicates that this participation is not passively experienced. It requires the choice to act with an openness to the divine presence when and where it has caused itself to be found. That is why God does not regularly perform these mighty acts. For those who deny God's providential power, even such regular performance would be wasted. Their obstinacy would block any message from ever coming through.[32] For those who do have a basic propensity for faith, the very activation of their faith demands that they be required to participate symbolically in these mighty acts, and not just wait for them to happen. Thus in writing about the "trial" of Abraham, Nahmanides points out the importance of one's faith being active rather than merely being potential of which one is only conscious:

> A trial (*nisayon*) is called such because of the one who is tried, but the one who tries him, may he be exalted, commands it in order to bring the matter from potentiality to actuality so that the one tried might get the reward due action, not just the reward for having a good heart ... and so indeed it is with all the trials that are in the Torah; they are for the good of the one who is tried.[33]

At the level of the historically based commandments, the needs being fulfilled are human needs. Here they are still similar to the commandments based on nature, the *mishpatim*. The latter fulfill the needs of humans in their relationships with one another in society; the former fulfill the needs of humans in their relationship with God in history. Ordinary people require the experience of the spectacular *public* miracles, either directly or symbolically, in order to appreciate God's transcendence of the natural order and their own capacity for transcending it too. In terms of Nahmanides' theological predecessors, his view of nature minus Aristotelian metaphysics comes closest to the view of Saadia Gaon (d. 942), and his view of the importance of history comes closest to the view of Judah Halevi (d. ca. 1140). Indeed, he was quite explicit in his acknowledgment of Halevi's influence on him.[34]

The Metasocial/Metahistorial Commandments

The commandments of the Torah designated as *huqqim*, "statutes," have always posed a special challenge to those who are committed to the view that *all* the commandments of the Torah have reasons, for these commandments seem to be arbitrary expressions of God's will. As one seminal midrash put it, God in effect says to the people of Israel, "I have enacted a statute (*huqqah haqqaqti*), I have decreed a decree (*gezerah gazarti*), and you are not permitted to transgress my decrees!"[35] Indeed, another midrash actually generalized from the *huqqim* and assumed that *all* the commandments (*ha-mitzvot*) were only given to test humanity's willingness to subordinate itself to God's will rather than to its own reason.[36] That is why the rabbis emphasized that Satan and the nations of the world taunt the Jewish people for their irrational tenaciousness in faithfully keeping these mysterious commandments.[37]

It is obvious, then, that those who affirm that all of the commandments of the Torah do have reasons, however obscure those reasons might at times be, will have to be able to plausibly suggest what at least some of these reasons are, especially for the problematic *huqqim*. If this cannot be done, it would seem more probable that either all of the commandments are in essence divine decrees and nothing more, or that even when there do seem to be reasons for some of the commandments, these "reasons" are only secondary surmisals of the meaning of these particular commandments rather than primary indications of their essential truth.[38] Both Maimonides and Nahmanides, being committed to the assumption of reasons for all the commandments respectively, developed means for explaining these difficult commandments. And, at this level of exegetical challenge, their fundamental theological differences are most apparent. Indeed, it is against the background of Maimonides' treatment of these commandments that Nahmanides' position becomes clearer by contrast.

For Maimonides, both truth and value are discovered in reality as understood by political science, physical science, or metaphysics. Clearly, his theology emphasizes the primacy of those commandments whose purposes are most evident to human reason *per se*, that is, the commandments dealing with the ordering of society towards what is good (*mishpatim*), or the ordering of the intellect towards what is true (*de'ot*). The historical commandments (*edot*) are seen too as functioning within this basic context. Thus the purpose of the observance of the Sabbath and festivals is for the political purpose of friendship through mutual rest and celebration and for the intellectual purpose of appreciating truths about the created cosmos.[39] History, as the appreciation of God's revelation through unique events, is not a consideration for Maimonides even when it would seem to be especially called for.[40]

Maimonides does invoke history, however, when explaining some of the *huqqim*. Here he sees some of them as having been enacted in reaction to certain manifestations of idolatry in ancient times.[41] Thus, concerning the prohibition of eating meat cooked in milk, Maimonides gives two reasons. First, he sees the high fat content of such food as being physically unhealthy. And, second, he surmises that such an act might well have been a pagan rite which the Torah did not want the people of Israel to imitate in any way.[42] Finally, as for the objection as to why a reaction to a no longer extant pagan rite still should be normative, it should be remembered that Maimonides saw the propensity for idolatry to be perpetual. Hence, even prohibitions against its particular temporal manifestations still serve the function of emphasizing how important perpetual diligence against this ever-probable general spiritual disease is.[43]

We see, then, that for Maimonides, the rationally evident commandments are primary, the explicitly historical commandments are in effect dehistoricized, and the mysterious *huqqim* are seen as reactions to historical manifestations of idolatry. Thus, it would seem that in his ordering of the commandments, the *mishpatim* (understood in both the political and intellectual sense) come first, the *edot* come second, and the *huqqim* come third in importance.

For Nahmanides, in stark opposition, the order would seem to be reversed, namely, the *mishpatim* are least important, the *edot* are more important, and the *huqqim*—precisely because of their mysterious quality—are the most important. This becomes more apparent when we see that it is in his explanations of the *huqqim* that Nahmanides invokes the authority of what he considers to be the true, that is, the deepest, teaching of the Torah—Kabbalah.

Nahmanides' invocation of Kabbalah has long been a subject of debate among scholars. On the one hand, scholars of a highly traditionalist stripe, who literally believe that the Zohar is the work of the second-century Tanna Rabbi Simon bar Yohai, and that it was always known as esoteric doctrine to certain chosen persons long before its publication in the thirteenth century, therefore believe that Nahmanides' invocation of Kabbalah is selective, that is, he knew a lot more than he actually revealed in his writings.[44] This view is consistent with the fact that kabbalists frequently claim that the very esoteric nature of Kabbalah requires such cryptic restraint. However, this view does not satisfactorily explain just why some kabbalistic doctrine was revealed and some was not, or why what was revealed is virtually always used to explain the reasons for *huqqim*. On the other hand, scholars of a more modern stripe almost always follow the widely accepted theory of Gershom Scholem that the Zohar is largely the work of Rabbi Moses de Leon, who wrote *after* Nahmanides and who was influenced *by* him.[45] As such, they usually argue that the sporadic nature of Nahmanides' invocation of Kabbalah is because his own kabbalistic theology is not nearly as systematic as that of de Leon and his successors.[46]

I would place myself in the modernist camp on this particular question of the temporal relation between the writings of Nahmanides and the Zohar. Furthermore, that there is nothing to suggest that Nahmanides' kabbalism was actually a systematic theology. Moreover, it should be emphasized that, unlike later kabbalists, beginning with de Leon and his successors, Nahmanides never attempted to explain everything in the Torah in the light of Kabbalah. Unlike the later kabbalists, he emphasized the reality of both nature and history when he thought that this was the best assumption for explaining a particular commandment or event in the Torah. Indeed, as we have already seen, in his use of nature for explaining the *mishpatim*, he very much approximates Saadia Gaon's theory of *rational* commandments, and in his use of history for explaining the *edot*, he is very much influenced by Judah Halevi's theory of unique events.

It would seem, then, that the place for one to invoke Kabbalah, when one does regard it as *the Truth* but not *all* the truth of the Torah, is in explaining the *huqqim*, which seem to have so little reference to either nature or history. In other words, his invocation of Kabbalah is consistent with the profound conservatism he frequently exhibits in both his halakhic and theological writings.[47] Kabbalah is not brought in to totally revolutionize Jewish theology on every point; rather it is brought in to explain what earlier theologies had either not explained at all, or what they had explained inadequately. As such, the *huqqim*, by their very mysterious character, offered the best field of Torah data for which Kabbalah could provide a needed theory of explanation.

It was in connection with the whole institution of sacrificial worship that many of the *huqqim* are presented. At the very beginning of his comments on the Book of Leviticus, the book of the Torah which deals most fully with the sacrificial system, Nahmanides objects to Maimonides' historicization of the whole institution, thus relativizing its importance:

> Maimonides in the *Guide of the Perplexed* said that the reason for the sacrifices is because the Egyptians and the Chaldeans, in whose land Israel had dwelled, had always worshipped cattle and sheep [and goats].... Because of this he commanded them to slaughter these three species to the Revered Name in order that it be known that what they had thought was the epitome of sin is that which they should now offer to the Creator.... And so will the bad beliefs, which are diseases of the soul, be cured, for every disease and every sickness is only cured by its opposite. —These are his words in which he spoke at length, but they are words of exaggeration.[48]

Nahmanides then offers two explanations which better account for the importance the Torah obviously ascribes to the sacrificial system. The first is a psychological one. It asserts that the sacrifices satisfy the profound human need to be reconciled with God in thought, in word, and in deed. Nahmanides accepts this interpretation as one which is immediately attractive to the imagination, one which "draws the heart."[49] Nevertheless, immediately after stating that, he alludes to the *true*, kabbalistic view, which emphasizes that the unique name of God (YHWH), and not the lesser names of God, is always mentioned in connection with the sacrifices. Hence, in explicitly direct contrast with Maimonides, Nahmanides raises what the former had relegated to the level of historical contingency to something immediately related to the very life of God.

The major difference in Nahmanides' use of kabbalistic interpretations for the commandments and his use of non-kabbalistic interpretations for them concerns his assignment of the essential reasons (that is, purposes) for the respective commandments. In the case of the social commandments (*mishpatim*) and the historical commandments (*edot*), the respective reason assigned is always one determined by human need. Human beings need laws to govern their social relationships. Jews need to commemorate the great historical events when God's power and providence were so unmistakably manifest to Israel. However, in the case of the *huqqim*, especially the positive precepts pertaining to the Temple and its cult, this is not the essential teleology at work. Thus commenting on the verse "And they shall know that I am the Lord their God who brought them out of the land of Egypt to dwell (*le-shokhni*) in their midst" (Exod. 29:46), Nahmanides writes:

> There is in this matter a great mystical teaching (*sod gadol*). For according to the ostensive meaning of the matter (*ke-fi peshat*) the presence of the Shekhinah is a human need (*tzorekh hedyot*) and not a divine need (*tzorekh gaboha*), but the topic is [rather] like the verse "Oh Israel, it is you in whom I glorify myself" [Isaiah 49:3].[50]

The subject of divine need is one which very much occupied the thought of kabbalists after Nahmanides.[51] Some went so far as to see the very emanation of the multifold world from the divine Oneness as the result of divine need for an "other."[52] Nahmanides' thought would not seem to mean something that radical, denying as it does the source of divine emanation and divine creation in divine freedom. Although, as is usually the case when he invokes kabbalistic doctrine, he does not elaborate on this doctrine, it would seem to mean for him that *since* God has chosen to substantially extend himself into multifold reality, he has *thereby* made himself dependent on it *insofar* as he is present in it. Of course, God as the wholly transcendent infinite (*En Sof*) is never wholly dependent on what participates in his life precisely because he is never *wholly* present in it. Thus, for example, in his introduction to his *Commentary on the Torah*, Nahmanides emphatically asserts the kabbalistic doctrine that the sanctity of the Torah is because its words are all permutations of the various names of God.[53] In that sense, God is present in the Torah and thus *needs* it. However, God is always more than his names; indeed, the *En Sof* (the "in-finite") is a negative term and, as such, God is essentially nameless at this level. Therefore, what Nahmanides seems to mean by *divine need* is that by doing the commandments, especially the mysterious *huqqim*, Jews are not passive recipients of God's grace given to beings essentially external to himself. Rather, they are now seen as essentially active participants in the internal life of God, an internal life where the various participants are mutually interrelated, that is, need each other. In retrospect, this aspect of Nahmanides' kabbalistic theology probably had the greatest influence on subsequent kabbalistic theology.[54]

So far, we have seen how Nahmanides' invocation of Kabbalah enabled him to offer a radically different view of the positive *huqqim* from that of earlier rationalist theologians like Maimonides. Although one can always debate the actual truth of his kabbalistic interpretations of the positive *huqqim*, they do, nevertheless, offer a much richer interpretation of them than Jewish rationalism could offer. It is thus not hard to see why they satisfied subsequent Jewish spiritual needs for understanding the purposes of the commandments much more than the earlier (and subsequent) rationalist interpretations did. However, Nahmanides did not limit himself to explaining the positive *huqqim* along these lines. The negative *huqqim* also called for similar interpretation. In explaining them, it will be recalled, Maimonides attempted to see these *huqqim* as proscribing what are essentially violations of natural law, that is, they proscribe violations of an order which is not invented by human reason but, rather, discovered by it. Like the *mishpatim* and the *edot*, the *huqqim* are ultimately explainable within the context of intelligible nature. For Nahmanides, too, these *huqqim* proscribe the violation of an order which is not invented by human reason. But for him, it is not an order which is discovered by human reason either. Rather, the *huqqim* proscribe the violation of the order created by God, but that aspect of this created order which is not discoverable by human reason, whose proper intentionality can only be revealed. As such, these laws are fundamentally different from the rationally evident *mishpatim*. Moreover, since their reasons are not explainable by public historical events, they are fundamentally different from the *edot*. Therefore, their purposes can only be seen when there is revealed to us something of the created order which is beyond both ordinary human reason and even extraordinary human experience. This comes out, especially, when Nahmanides explains the reasons for the most perplexing of the negative *huqqim*, those which prohibit the crossbreeding of different species of animals. In commenting on the verse "You shall keep my statutes (*et huqqotai*): you shall not crossbreed species" (Lev. 19:19), Nahmanides writes:

> The *huqqim* are the decree of the king (*gezerat ha-melekh*) which he has decreed (*yihoq*) in his kingdom without revealing their purpose (*to'eletam*) to the people…. The person who crossbreeds species

changes and falsifies the very work of creation; it is as if he thinks that God did not satisfactorily fulfill (*she-lo hishlim*) every need (*kol tzorekh*).[55]

This act and those like it are seen as basically denying the fulfillment of the created needs of ordinary earthly creatures. They can be seen as tampering with the created order and thus asserting that God has not satisfactorily finished his task of creation, that human beings can essentially improve upon it and thus truly complete it. The proscription, then, is for the sake of asserting that God's creation is perfect even though ordinary human reason frequently does not understand how God's providence operates in creation. Such a true understanding of the ways of providence must wait for the type of esoteric revelation which someone like Job finally received directly from God.[56]

Finally, this proscription of changing the higher created order by attempting to manipulate it, even if the intent here is to improve it, is in essence a proscription of magic. Here again, contrasting Nahmanides' view with that of Maimonides is helpful for understanding the deeper meaning of his theological position.

For Maimonides, magic is proscribed not because it is objectively efficacious, but because it is subjectively dangerous.[57] Magic distorts the human subject's understanding of the true operations of the natural order, operations discernible through scientific demonstration, not superstitious opinion. Human action cannot possibly have any real effect on the perpetual natural order, let alone on the wholly transcendent life of God. But for Nahmanides, on the other hand, magic is indeed efficacious. Its proscription is not because it is untrue, but because it is an evil attempt to ultimately control God for human advantage.[58] Such evil human action can indeed upset the order of creation itself, perhaps even temporarily thwart the fulfillment of divine needs, but never to the extent that it can overturn divine omnipotence within creation. Thus, even though human actions can be seen as fulfilling inner divine needs, this does not mean that humans can act as if they have actual control over God. It seems that in the ultimate scheme of things, it is God himself who enables his inner needs to be fulfilled. Human power is only ultimately real when it is a faithful participation in the life God is already living.

Conclusion

Nahmanides' *Commentary on the Torah*, which is his *magnum opus*, summarizing and developing ideas present in his earlier writings, indeed contains a systematic Jewish theology. Many students of his commentary have failed to see that system because they have looked for a *wholly* kabbalistic systematic theology there. Accepting Nahmanides' own explicit assertions that Kabbalah is *the truth* of the Torah, they have assumed that Nahmanides must have regarded it as *all* the truth of the Torah. However, as we have seen in examining his treatment of the reasons for the commandments of the Torah, he also finds the truth of the Torah as involving the reality of nature and the reality of history. It is Kabbalah, though, which is the highest level of Torah truth, and it is the truth which places all other truth in a proper hierarchy and perspective. Hence, Kabbalah itself is not wholly sufficient to explain the Torah, but it is wholly necessary for there to be any systematic theology adequate to the Torah and the Judaism built upon it.

Nahmanides' *Commentary on the Torah*, then, is surely a *great* Jewish book because it has become indispensable for understanding the relationship of the Jewish people and the Torah. It has not only become a permanent element of the Jewish past, but it has remained a permanent element of the Judaism of the present. Even though one cannot present a totally Nahmanidean Jewish theology today (or that of any earlier Jewish thinker), one which could adequately deal with many of the spiritual and intellectual needs of contemporary Jews, still one cannot present any such theology which does not seriously consider many of Nahmanides' insights and positions, and which does not incorporate at least some of them. His theology cannot be ignored or slighted. The greatness of this Jewish book is still its indispensability—even across a time span of seven centuries—for understanding our relationship with the Torah in the context of our own Jewish life today.

The Solomon Goldman Lectures

All translations are by the author.
1. See *New Republic*, 4 April 1988, 28ff. for a full discussion of this whole controversy.
2. *The Republic of Plato* (New York, 1968).
3. The political significance of this practice was first emphasized by Josephus, *Contra Apionem*, 2.175; also, see *Antiquities*, 16.43.
4. See Rashbam, *Commentary on the Torah* to Gen. 37:2 re *Baba Metzia* 33a. Cf. Moses Schreiber, *Responsa Hatam Sofer*, "Yoreh Deah," no. 254.
5. See, e.g., *Baba Kama* 41b re Deut. 10:20 (the statement of Simon Ha-Amsoni).
6. Thus, the principle "Scripture speaks about its own present time (*be-hoveh*)" is used to explain why certain entities are mentioned in a particular Scriptural law. But the law is not then seen as being limited to them; rather, they are seen as being *examples* of a general class which includes a potentially infinite number of other examples. As such, what seems to be an assertion of self-sufficient *peshat* is, actually, a basis for *derash*. See, e.g., *M. Baba Kama* 5:7; also, *Encyclopedia Talmudit*, 6:553-555. Furthermore, the rabbinic principle "Scripture does not depart from its ostensive meaning (*midei peshuto*)" was not interpreted to foreclose *derash*, but to give it a basis. See *Yebamot* 24a and parallels; *Midrash Leqah Tob*, "Vayetzei," ed. Buber, 72b-73a.
7. Franz Rosenzweig aptly expressed this when he wrote to Jakob Rosenheim in 1927: "Uns ist die Ergaenzung der Einheit des geschriebenen Buchs durch die Einheit des gelesenen.... Wie dort die Einheit der Lehre, so erfaehrt er hier die Einheit des Lernens, des eigenen Lernens mit dem Lernen der Jahrhunderte. Die Tradition ... wird selber ein Element der Uebersetzung." Franz Rosenzweig, *Die Schrift*, ed. K. Thieme (Koenigstein, 1984), 29-30.
8. See I. Heinemann, *Ta'amei Ha-Mitzvot be-Sifrut Yisrael* (Jerusalem, 1957), 1:11ff.
9. See Israel Meir Ha-Kohen, *Mishnah Berurah* on *Shulhan Arukh*, "Orah Hayyim," 60.4, n. 11.
10. Originally, *kavvanat ha-leb,* in this sense, only applied to the commandment of reciting the first verse of the Shema and the Shemonah Esreh. See *M. Berakhot* 2:1; *Sifre* "Debarim," no. 41; also, David Weiss Halivni, *Meqorot u-Mesorot: Mo'ed/Yoma—Hagigah* (Jerusalem, 1975), 404-405. However, eventually *kavvanat ha-leb* was seen as the desideratum for all *mitzvot*. See, esp., Nahmanides' note on Maimonides, *Sefer Ha-Mitzvot*, pos. no. 5.
11. See *God in Search of Man* (New York, 1955), 320ff.
12. *Commentary on the Torah* (hereafter "CT"), ed. C. B. Chavel (Jerusalem, 1959), Lev. 19:2.
13. See, e.g., *Two Types of Faith*, trans. N. P. Goldhawk (London, 1961), 57. For a critique of Buber on this point, see David Novak, *Jewish-Christian Dialogue: A Jewish Justification* (New York, 1989), 89-91.
14. As precedent for this view, viz., that the search for the reasons for the commandments should only lead to better observance of them, not to their neglect, see Philo, *Migration of Abraham*, 89-93; Maimonides, "Hilkhot Teshubah," 3:4.
15. *Guide*, III, 27.
16. Ibid., III, 48. See David Novak, *Law and Theology in Judaism* (New York, 1978), 40ff.
17. See Maimonides, "Hilkhot Yesodei Ha-Torah," 4:13; *Guide*, II, 33.
18. See C. B. Chavel, *Rabbenu Mosheh ben Nahman* (Jerusalem, 1967), 120ff.

19. See, e.g., CT, Exod. 20:23. For Nahmanides' scheme of the classification of the *mitzvot*, see C. Henoch, *Ha-Ramban Ke-Hoqer u-Mequbbal* (Jerusalem, 1978), 337ff.

20. Against this whole line of interpretation, see David Berger, "Miracles and the Natural Order in Nahmanides" in *Rabbi Moses Nahmanides (Ramban): Explorations in His Religious and Literary Virtuosity*, ed. I. Twersky (Cambridge, Mass., 1983), 107ff.

21. *T. Abodah Zarah* 8:4; *Sanhedrin* 56a-b.

22. See Saadia Gaon, *Emunot ve-De'ot* 9:2, re Gen. 2:16; also, David Novak, *The Image of the Non-Jew in Judaism: An Historical and Constructive Study of the Noahide Laws* (New York and Toronto, 1983), esp. chap. 10.

23. "Hilkhot Melakhim," 8:11. See Novak, *Image of the Non-Jew*. op. cit.

24. *Shemonah Peraqim*, chap. 6.

25. David Novak, "Law and Ethics in Maimonides' Theology," *Solomon Goldman Lectures* (Chicago, 1982), 3:11ff.

26. CT, Gen. 6:13. See ibid., 6:2.

27. CT, Exod. 12:21.

28. See, e.g., CT, Deut. 13:2.

29. CT, Exod. 13:16.

30. For useful discussion of this point of view, see W. H. Walsh, *Philosophy of History: An Introduction*, rev. ed. (New York and Evanston, 1960), 63ff.

31. See Mircea Eliade, *The Sacred and the Profane: The Nature of Religion* (New York, 1961), 106-107.

32. See CT, Gen. 14:10.

33. CT, Gen. 22:1.

34. See CT, Deut. 11:22.

35. *Bemidbar Rabbah* 19:1. Cf. *Midrash Leqah Tob,* "Huqqat," 119b.

36. *Bereshit Rabbah* 44:1 and parallels.

37. *Sifra,* "Aharei Mot," ed. Weiss, 86a; *Yoma* 67b.

38. See David Novak, "Natural Law, Halakhah and the Covenant," *The Jewish Law Annual* (1988) 7:47ff.

39. *Guide*, III, 43.

40. See David Novak, "Does Maimonides Have a Philosophy of History?" in *Studies in Jewish Philosophy: Collected Essays of the Academy for Jewish Philosophy 1980-1985*, ed. N. M. Samuelson (Lanham, Md., 1989), 397ff.

41. *Guide*, III, 37.

42. Ibid., III, 48. See "Hilkhot Ma'akhalot Asurot," 17:29-31; also, "Hilkhot De'ot," 3:3 re Abot 2:2.

43. See, e.g., *Guide*, I, 36; III, 29.

44. See, e.g., J. Even-Chen, *Ha-Ramban* (Jerusalem, 1976), 61ff. Cf. Gershom Scholem, *Ha-Kabbalah be-Gerona* (Jerusalem, 1964), 73ff. and *Origins of the Kabbalah*, ed. R. J. Z. Werblowsky (Philadelphia and Princeton, 1987), 384; also, Moshe Idel, *Kabbalah: New Perspectives* (New Haven, 1988), 254.

45. See *Major Trends in Jewish Mysticism*, 3rd rev. ed. (New York, 1961), 173.

46. See Moshe Idel, "We Have No Kabbalistic Tradition on This" in *Rabbi Moses Nahmanides*, 63ff.

47. See his "Introduction to Notes on the Enumeration of the Commandments," *Kitvei Ramban*, ed. C. B. Chavel (Jerusalem, 1963), 1:420; also, Scholem, *Origins of the Kabbalah*, 389.

48. CT, Lev. 1:9, re *Guide*, III, 46.

49. Re *Shabbat* 87a and *Hagigah* 14a.

50. CT, Exod. 29:46.

51. See, e.g., Meir ibn Gabbai, *Abodat Ha-Qodesh*, 2:2ff.

52. See, e.g., Hayyim Vital, *Etz Hayyim*, 1:11a.

53. Thus C. B. Chavel, following the strictly traditionalist view that the Zohar is a *source* for Nahmanides, sees the source (*meqoro*) of this doctrine in the Zohar, "Yitro," 2:87a (see CT, Introduction, ed. Chavel, 6, note thereon). Actually, it is much more plausible to see Nahmanides as the Zohar's source for this basic kabbalistic doctrine. For the use of this theological point as the deeper meaning of the halakhic norm that a *sefer Torah* which is in anywise defective is invalid for the public reading of the Torah in the synagogue (see Maimonides, "Hilkhot Sefer Torah," 10:1, nos. 12 and 13), see Abraham ben Yom Tob Ishbili, *Responsa ha-Ritba*, ed. Kafih (Jerusalem, 1959), 167-70, no. 142 (in the name of Nahmanides, not the Zohar!).

54. The most profound restatement of this kabbalistic doctrine of the interaction of divine and human needs was made by my late revered teacher, Abraham Joshua Heschel. See his *Man is Not Alone* (Philadelphia, 1951), 241ff.

55. See, also, CT, Lev. 26:15.

56. See Nahmanides' comment on Job 42:5 in *Kitvei Ramban*, 1:126.

57. See "Hilkhot Abodah Zarah," 11:16; also, *Commentary on the Mishnah*, "Pesahim" 4:10.

58. See, e.g., CT, Exod. 8:14.

Gersonides' Place in the History of Philosophy
by
Norbert M. Samuelson

The purpose of this study is to present a general assessment of the importance of Gersonides' writings, not merely for Jewish philosophy but for philosophy in general. There are two factors to be considered in such a judgment. The first has to do with intellectual history. Who influenced Gersonides' thought and whom did he influence? The second is a question of philosophy. What did he say that was unique and how "good " is it? "Good" in this case is a quality judgment that in itself involves assessment of two distinct factors. First, how skilled was he as a philosopher? "Skill" in this case has to do with the degree of precision and depth of his writings. Second, is what he uniquely said true? This second aspect of the second question is the most important consideration. A negative answer in this case makes Gersonides' thought, no matter how influential or technically skilled it is, nothing more than a datum of a now dead past, whereas a positive answer makes his writings a philosophical classic, i.e., something that deserves serious contemplation by all serious philosophers both now and in the future as well.

Gersonides' Place in Western Intellectual History

In our present century there are three primary centers for philosophy—Great Britain, continental Western Europe (primarily Germany and France), and the United States. The dominant tradition of Great Britain can be called "analytic philosophy." Its sources are in the beginning of this century in the ideal language philosophy of Bertrand Russell and in the ordinary language philosophy of the later writings of Ludwig Wittgenstein. The dominant tradition of the continent can be called "existentialism." Its source, also around the beginning of this century, is the phenomenology of Edmund Husserl. For the most part, American philosophy has been either analytic or phenomenological. In general, the current seat for analytic philosophy is in university philosophy departments, while existentialism tends to be studied in religion departments. However, there is also a distinct tradition of American philosophy. It can be called "radical empiricism." Its sources, again around the beginning of this century, are the pragmatism of C. S. Peirce, William James and John Dewey, as well as the process philosophy of Alfred North Whitehead.

What all three contemporary traditions of Western philosophy share is that they are all in significantly different ways reactions against the philosophy of Hegel. In both the British and the American cases, the Hegelianism rejected was that of F. H. Bradley and Bernard Bosanquet. In the case of the continent, the revolt against Hegel began in the second half of the nineteenth century in the so-called "new philosophy" of Soren Kierkegaard, Arthur Schopenhauer and Friedrich Nietzsche.

Hegel's philosophy in itself is one of three major philosophical traditions in Germany that grew out of the thought of Immanuel Kant. The other two are those of Friedrich von Schelling and Hermann Cohen. The Cohen tradition, commonly called "Marburg neo-Kantianism," is of particular interest for understanding the sources of contemporary continental philosophy. At present, intellectual life on the continent (as well as in many American religion departments) is dominated by a form of thought commonly called "hermeneutics." Its most important representatives are the French philosophers Jacques Derrida and his teacher, Emmanuel Levinas. Levinas' primary philosophic influences are Martin Heidegger (whose primary teacher was Husserl) and Franz Rosenzweig (whose teacher was Cohen).

In each of these cases the primary influences were negative, but, nonetheless, they remain primary influences. Heidegger's philosophy was built on what he rejected from his teacher Husserl, as Rosenzweig's was on his rejection of the doctrines of Cohen, all of whom based their thought on rejecting the affirmations of Hegel. Still, Hegel, Husserl and Cohen remain their most important intellectual sources. The situation is like an adult son who models his role as a parent on not being like his father. The only way he knows how to father is the way his father fathered him, and he knows that his own father did not do a good job. Hence, the only way he knows how to father is *not* to be like his own father. As such, his father, albeit negatively, is his sole role model. Similarly, the tradition of positive philosophy, from Kant, through Hegel and Cohen, to Heidegger and Levinas, is the primary source for contemporary continental philosophy, albeit the influence is often negative. All of which brings us back to Kant as the critical shared link for every branch of continental philosophy.

Kant's philosophy has two roots. One (the minor one) is the tradition of British empiricism, from (in reverse order) David Hume, George Berkeley and John Locke. Two (the major one) is the tradition of continental rationalism, whose source is the thought of the contemporaries Baruch Spinoza and Gottfried Leibniz. Of the latter two, the influence of the thought of Spinoza was more comprehensive. Beyond their shared influence in traditional philosophic subjects such as ontology and metaphysics, Leibniz's influence is unquestionably more important for the subsequent development of the physical sciences and formal logic. On the other hand, no single source was more significant than Spinoza's writings for subsequent modern thought in the broad range of human sciences—including religion, biblical criticism, politics and ethics.

Most courses in the history of philosophy in English-speaking countries will identify the source of Spinoza's thought in that of René Descartes, whose own dominant, albeit negative, influences were the Christian scholastics. It should by now be clear to any rigorous student of the history of ideas that this genealogy of conceptual influences on Western thought is without any foundation. The seminal work in this regard was Harry Wolfson's *The Philosophy of Spinoza* (Cambridge, 1934). Wolfson demonstrated that whatever impact the tradition of Christian scholasticism and Descartes had on Spinoza, the primary sources for his thought were the major figures of medieval Jewish philosophy.

That most contemporary philosophers in Britain and the United States have ignored Wolfson's findings has more to do with academic politics and their own ignorance than any weakness in the argumentation of this Wolfson masterpiece. It is reasonable for a scholar to deal only with what he knows and to avoid what he does not know. If the sources of Spinoza's thought are Descartes and the Christian scholastics, then the traditional education of most Anglo-American philosophers would equip them to read and discuss Spinoza's thought. However, if Wolfson is right (which undoubtedly he is), then to read Spinoza, it is not enough to read French and Latin; Hebrew and Arabic are required. Similarly, it is not enough to be exposed to Descartes, and the likes of Aquinas, Scotus and Occam. The informed scholar must also know the thought of the likes of Al-Farabi, Ibn Sina, Maimonides, Gersonides and Crescas. Now, such knowledge never was included in the classical curriculum of Oxford and Cambridge, let alone in the philosophy departments of even the leading American universities. Hence, scholars trained in these institutions must either return to school to be re-educated or ignore Spinoza altogether. The former alternative is too difficult for most professors of philosophy, even if they were willing to acknowledge this major lacuna in their education, and the latter alternative is not possible, given the generally acknowledged central role that Spinoza plays in the historical development of all Western thought. Hence, either out of ignorance or guile, most students of Western intellectual history, including several renowned Spinoza scholars, have ignored Wolfson's findings and, in consequence, ignored the real sources of Spinoza's thought.

The intent of this excursion in intellectual genealogy has been to assert the importance of the thought of Gersonides for the history of philosophy in Western civilization. I have traced the development of Western philosophy backwards from the major varieties of contemporary philosophy (as they are discussed in departments of philosophy and religion) to their sources in medieval philosophy. It remains to move forward from Gersonides' place in the genealogy of medieval philosophy in order to establish his role in molding contemporary philosophy.

In the Muslim world a new science, rooted in the writings of Aristotle, arose at the end of the twelfth century, which supplanted the older atomistic scientific tradition of the Mutakallimun. At first Aristotelian thought was limited to the physical sciences. There persisted a radical discontinuity between the way people thought about subjects like optics, botany, biology, astronomy, etc., and the way they thought about the human sciences of religion, political theory and ethics. In this respect, the twelfth century in the Muslim world was a time not unlike our own, where humanists and theologians seem quite content to pursue their speculation as if the world were still the kind of place that Newton described in his classical mechanistic physics, in almost total ignorance of the new, more relativistic physics of Einstein, Heisenberg, Schrodinger and Bohr.

The initial major step in integrating the new, Aristotelian physical science with the humanities was Abraham ibn Daud's (1110-1180) *The Exalted Faith*.[1] In the first part of his masterpiece, Ibn Daud summarized the basic picture of the universe, and in the rest of the book he used his initial summary to reinterpret the truth claims of rabbinic Judaism. Parallel efforts of integration took place in Muslim society in the various works of Al-Farabi and Ibn Sina (Avicenna). This effort to present a coherent view of the universe that unified both the physical and the humanistic sciences culminated at the end of the twelfth century in the writings of the Muslim Ibn Rushd (Averroes) and the Jew Moses ibn Maimon (Maimonides).

It was the writings of Averroes and Maimonides that provided the fundamental understanding of the then-called "new science" that the Christian scholastics used to redefine their thirteenth and fourteenth-century view of God's universe. However, their struggle to attain positive knowledge was by no means confined to reading ancient texts. While texts served as the focus for their speculation, these scholastics went beyond any mere slavish adherence to their tradition. On the contrary, they struggled with these texts not so much to be able to understand the historic intent of these (by now considered) ancient wise men, but, through their guidance, to discover the truth. Nor was this speculation carried out by Christian monks in isolation. Jews as well, living in proximity to these centers of Christian learning, were also actively involved in their own reading of these texts for parallel reasons.

The two most important names of Christian scholastics in this period of absorption and integration were Thomas Aquinas (1225-1274) and John Duns Scotus (ca. 1266-1308). Their Jewish counterparts were Gersonides (Levi ben Gerson, 1288-1344) and Hasdai Crescas (1340-1410). Based on overt, explicit statements by these philosophers, we know that for all of them the primary sources for their philosophy were Maimonides and Averroes. Similarly, we know that Duns Scotus was influenced by Aquinas and Crescas by Gersonides.

At the same time there are no comparable statements to show that Gersonides read Aquinas or that Crescas read Scotus. However, intellectual historians of the period have little doubt that this was the case.[2]

To summarize, a proper genealogy of intellectual influences from the twelfth century to the present would produce the chart given at the end of this essay. In terms of historical influence on contemporary Western thought, those philosophers whose work was specifically Jewish who had the greatest influence were Ibn Daud, Maimonides, Gersonides, Crescas, Spinoza, Hermann Cohen, Franz Rosenzweig and Emmanuel Levinas. Ibn Daud and Maimonides began the process of applying Aristotelian categories of thought to medieval religious and political thought, which culminated in the critical studies of both Gersonides and Crescas. Gersonides and Crescas represent medieval Aristotelianism at its technical best as it influenced the thought of Spinoza, who, together with Leibniz, set the basic directions for Western philosophy into the contemporary world of British language analysis, American process philosophy and continental existentialism.

Gersonides' Place in Jewish Intellectual History

The intellectual life of thirteenth-century Europe was dominated by debates over the value of the new Aristotelian science for religious faith and ethics. In the case of the Christians, the debate focused on the consequences of applying Averroes' commentaries on Aristotle to a new understanding of epistemology and a reinterpretation of the relation between religious tradition rooted in revelation and empirical science based on human reason. In the case of the Jews, the argument focused on interpreting Maimonides' account of the rabbinic dogmas of Mosaic prophecy, divine providence, messianism and immortality.[3] The leading rabbis of Europe, for a variety of different motives,[4] took sides in the dispute. In general, most participants in this internal Jewish debate shared the following beliefs. First, Maimonides' personal faith commitment was undeniable. Secondly, when reason is properly used, it will recognize its appropriate limitations and never affirm any doctrines that contradict authentic rabbinic interpretation of the Mosaic revelation. Nevertheless, they disagreed about the value of such knowledge for Jews. Those who opposed the new science, such as Hasdai Crescas, maintained that this path to knowledge was so limited and filled with danger, that the mass of Jews would be better off avoiding it altogether. In fact, they argued, the path that led from the study of biblical commentaries to absorption in rabbinic law and codes was less dangerous, provided surer conviction, and yielded as much if not more positive knowledge. On the other hand, those who championed the new science, such as Gersonides, argued that a full, positive commitment to the faith of Israel can only be made secure to the extent that every tool of understanding that God, in his grace, made available to humanity is harnessed in the service of God. Those who rarely think may be satisfied with stories dictated by the imagination of political leaders. However, those whom God blessed with excellence of reason will not be able to restrain their passion to discover the deepest meanings of these myths in their unquenchable thirst for knowledge of the God of truth as it is revealed in the order of his created world.

The dispute between Gersonides, Israel's greatest champion of the value of scientific knowledge for faith, and Crescas, Israel's most important critic of this religious path, was modeled on the earlier literary exchange between the anti-rationalist Al-Ghazali and the rationalist Averroes. In both the Muslim and the Jewish cases, the opponents of natural science tended to be victorious. Both the Muslims and the Jews advocated three ways to serve and know God. For the greater mass of the community of the faithful the one available path was through law—*shariya* in the case of Islam and *halakhah* in the case of Judaism. For the elite who could fulfill the law but who sought more intimate, direct knowledge, there were other alternatives—the way of philosophy through the study of the natural sciences, and the way of mysticism through meditation. What in fact happened in both religious communities was that the desire of the few for philosophic/scientific knowledge became submerged into meditation and mysticism. For all of the faithful in both the Muslim and Jewish communities, law and only law became the sole authentic expression of religious faith, while both religious polities continued to tolerate the perceived indulgence of the few in mysticism—Sufism in the case of Islam and Kabbalah in the case of Judaism. However, at least in the case of Judaism, the desire for rational knowledge, while redirected, was not completely suppressed. It persisted in the Renaissance in a significant minority of rabbis who studied the new, post-Aristotelian, empirical sciences.[5] It was this (as yet largely unresearched) interest in empirical science that provided the continuity that enabled Spinoza to find in the writings of both Crescas and Gersonides the foundations for a new, modern, liberal approach to all of science, from physics and epistemology to biblical criticism, personal ethics, and political theory.

Gersonides as a Philosopher

So far my remarks on the importance of Gersonides have only been genealogical, without saying anything specific about what Gersonides wrote that gave him this place of prominence in Western intellectual history. Let me turn now to Gersonides' actual writings.[6]

In general, Gersonides followed the philosophical writings of Maimonides and Averroes, both of which he knew through Hebrew translations. His major philosophic work, *The Wars of the Lord*,[7] only dealt with issues on which he disagreed with their conclusions. These topics fall into six major categories, each of which corresponds to a different book of *The Wars*: (1) the immortality of the soul, (2) prophecy, (3) God's attributes and knowledge, (4) divine providence, (5) astronomy, and (6) creation. In each of these cases Gersonides' central theses are unique and of significant importance in the subsequent history of ideas. However, there is no space in a single essay to explain all of them. For the present, it will be enough to limit the discussion to what Gersonides said about divine attributes[8] in relation to the general state of "God-talk" within contemporary philosophy of religion.

While the word "God" has been used throughout Jewish history to name that entity who is most worthy of worship, it is far from clear that the entity named in each case is the same. Clearly, Jews have said radically different things about God, and there is no simple way to determine what their difference is. One possibility is that they are talking about the same entity, in which case they differ in their description of him. Even the use of the term "him" with reference to God is problematic, for at present there is a major controversy over the convention of using masculine terms to refer to God.[9] At the same time a second, even more serious possibility is that these Jews are talking about different entities. In the former case, if we assume that the deity described is in fact the God of Israel, at worst someone who is wrong is a heretic, but in the latter case someone who is wrong is guilty of idolatry, the most serious of all crimes from the perspective of both the Hebrew Scriptures and rabbinic tradition.

Traditionally, the God of the faith of Israel has been called both *"Adonai"* and *"Elohim,"* and referred to as both the deity of Abraham, Isaac, and Jacob and as the creator of the world. Again, traditionally these two names and two references have been identified, i.e., *Adonai* is *Elohim* who is both the creator of the universe and the deity of the Bible's patriarchs and matriarchs. However, this identity is not self-evident. If we exclude the authority of the arguments of medieval Aristotelian philosophers who were committed Muslims, Jews or Christians, it could be the case that they are not the same and/or that one but not the other or neither of them exists.

For the sole purpose of simplicity, let us reserve the term *"Elohim"* for the purported creator of the universe, and the term *"Adonai"* for the deity associated by Scripture with the patriarchs and matriarchs. The claim that both exist and are one requires three distinct lines of demonstration. While most modern Jewish thinkers have made these three traditional claims, with or without demonstration, it is not true that all of them have. In fact some of the most interesting ones have not. Spinoza would affirm the existence of *Elohim* as the one absolutely infinite substance, but not the existence of *Adonai*. Conversely, Martin Buber spoke of *Adonai,* to the exclusion of *Elohim,* as the "Eternal-Thou."[10]

In any case, to ask if *Elohim* and *Adonai* exist and are the same referent presupposes some prior concept of what they are. In the case of *Adonai* this is a fairly easy question to answer. He is the author of the Torah. How he did so, for our present purposes, is unimportant.[11] It may be the case, as most contemporary Orthodox Jews believe, that the Torah that we possess today is the sole creation of that deity and that he transmitted it to Moses at Sinai some three thousand years ago. Or it may be the case, as many liberal religious Jews believe, that *Adonai* is a force that guided some or all of the Jewish people, who, through his influence, composed our Torah and attributed it to him. These questions of authorship are certainly of great importance, but again, they lie outside the scope of this essay. Our question is not, how did *Adonai* author the Torah; it is instead, who is its author.

Our question about *Adonai* is similar to asking what kind of person could write Shakespeare's plays rather than asking how Shakespeare's plays were written. The answer to the latter question could be that there was a single producer and director who composed all of the plays that his London company gave, or it could be that every play presented by the company had a different author but they were all called "Shakespeare's" because he was their producer. In contrast, an answer to the former question could be "someone loyal to Queen Elizabeth who had a Thomistic view of the heavens and enjoyed slap-stick comedy." In this sense *Adonai* is a person with a flexible body.[12] He is a "person" in that he can be the subject of mental acts and will actions. And his "body" is "flexible" in that he can appear in, at or through different kinds of physical objects, and that in fact there are no limitations on the kinds of physical forms that are associated with him, even though the ones that Scripture tends to mention involve fire and light in one way or another. In addition, he exhibits many characteristics that, while they need not be identical with human characteristics, are in a significant way similar to human qualities, such as loving and judging. Furthermore, whatever is the precise meaning of saying that *Adonai* loves and judges, he loves and judges different species of individual living things and different nations of human beings in different ways. In this rather vague sense it can be said that *Adonai* loves the nation of the people of Israel and he promises to preserve and prosper it. Furthermore, any entity of whom the above statements are not true is not the author of the Torah. This denial is logically comparable to saying that any person or persons who did not hold the views and did not have the artistic style of the author of Shakespeare's plays is not Shakespeare, no matter who Shakespeare was.

On the other hand, to ask who *Elohim* is is more difficult. In this case there is no single answer. Who *Adonai* is is defined by his relation to the Torah. While contemporary Jews disagree about how the Torah was written, there is no comparable problem in identifying the Torah. It is a certain commonly accepted set of writings in a form over which there is relatively minimal disagreement. Conversely, who *Elohim* is is defined by his relation to the universe, and it is far less clear what the world is. In fact there are as many different views of the universe as there are different systems of contemporary philosophy and physics. How *Elohim* is described differs radically depending on what kind of world we are discussing.

Historically, the tradition of classical Jewish and Christian philosophy that contemporary theologians have inherited synthesizes the philosophies of Plato and Aristotle, but these two philosophers proposed significantly different world views. The Platonic universe is a world of perfect ideals that have absolute existence and are related by some kind of theory of imitation to less perfect entities, that are subject to different degrees of existence/reality, depending on their different degrees of perfection. Conversely, the Aristotelian universe is a world of general forms whose existence is mental, that inhere in material entities that occupy three-dimensional space. At the same time, Newtonian physics posits an atomist universe of simple quantities that occupy multi-dimensional space.[13] Nor are these the only alternatives. Modern philosophers have constructed many different ontologies, and many of them have had an important impact on contemporary Jewish theology.

Anselm's world is one kind of Platonic universe, and at least two Jewish philosophers, viz. Philo and Solomon ibn Gabirol, shared Anselm's basic world view. The *Elohim* of such a universe is (a) something a greater than which cannot be conceived, (b) unlimited, (c) something whose existence and nonexistence is not merely logically possible, and (d) something that can neither come into existence nor cease to exist, but (e) something that necessarily exists.[14] Furthermore, we can stipulate logical rules that will determine *a priori* what attributions are and are not true of him. (1) No nongraded exclusion predicate can be affirmed of him.[15] (2) If any graded predicate is less than some other graded predicate, then the lesser predicate cannot be affirmed of him. (3) If predicating a graded predicate entails predicating a nongraded exclusion predicate of that thing, then the graded predicate in question cannot be predicated of him. (4) Concerning any graded predicate that does not entail a nongraded exclusion predicate, if that predicate expresses the highest perfection possible in its class, then that predicate is affirmed of him. (5) Concerning any class of predicates which are not exclusion predicates, if one member of that class of predicates is predicable of him, then all members of that class are predicable of him. Finally, (6) concerning any predicate which is not an exclusion predicate which does not entail a nongraded exclusion predicate, if it is predicable of anything, then it is predicated of him. In short, it is the *Elohim* whose existence Anselm demonstrated.

The above six logical rules that determine *a priori* what attributions are and are not true of the Platonic *Elohim* apply to the Aristotelian *Elohim*. However, to them must be added a seventh rule originally formulated by Gersonides. Given any predicate F that can be affirmed of God, F is applied primarily to God in an absolute sense and derivatively to anything else in a less than absolute sense that admits of degrees of perfection. Furthermore, if G, whose sense differs from F, can also be affirmed of God, then G and F have the same referent, namely, God. For example, God knows himself in a single act of knowledge that is identical with God, and in knowing himself he knows everything as its cause. In contrast, we know something through multiple acts as an effect of what exists through God's causation. Furthermore, in our case the following are all distinct: (a) each of us as the subject of the act of knowing, (b) our acts of knowing themselves, and (c) the objects of our knowledge. In these ways our knowledge is both dependent upon and inferior to God's knowledge.

Gersonides' formulation of divine attributes had a direct influence on how Spinoza understood the nature of God as an absolutely infinite substance. However, there are significant differences between Gersonides' theory of attributes and that of his predecessor Maimonides, who argued that literally no univocal affirmation is possible in a sentence whose subject is God. Rather, affirmative declarative sentences are possible in a language of "God-talk" only where those sentences are equivocal in meaning. What it means to say that God is F, where F is any predicate whose contrary is G, is that God is not G, F is a human excellence, and G is a human vice. In other words, on final analysis, statements about God do not inform us about God; rather they instruct us in human ethics as will soon become apparent.

Zevi Diesendruck, following in the philosophical tradition of Hermann Cohen, interpreted Maimonides' theory of negative attributes as an instance of Kantian infinite judgments.[16] According to Kant, judgments of the form "S is non-P" are not logically the same as judgments of the form "S is not P." The latter are negative statements whose form is finite, i.e., a specific predicate is being denied of a specific subject. However, the former statements are not only grammatically but logically affirmative, and in this case what is being affirmed is infinite, namely, a class containing an infinite number of members, each of which is a proper contrary of P. Here, to say that "S is not non-P" logically differs from making the affirmative, finite claim that "S is P." Rather, "S is not non-P" negates an infinite class of alternatives, and as such it yields some form of knowledge, even when the number of possible alternatives for positive predication is infinite. The sense in which the statement that an infinite series of individual acts of negation can express something positive turns on Cohen's application of the infinitesimal calculus to theology.

Consider the statement "God is F," where each $G_1, G_2, \ldots G_n, G_{n+1}, \ldots$ is a contrary of F. What this statement means is the following: Based on the dictum, "You shall be holy as I the Lord your God am holy," we are commanded to strive to become F. To be F lies beyond human capability; at best in this world we approximate this ideal by avoiding each of the infinite number of contraries of F that are not true of God. In this life this moral guide is how we relate to God.

It should be noted that the two primary interpretations of divine attributes in the Aristotelian version, viz. those of Maimonides and Gersonides, need not be viewed as mutually exclusive. In fact, Diesendruck's interpretation of Maimonides' theory of negative attributes might best be understood as a reconstruction of Maimonides' view in accordance with Gersonides' position. In this case both Jewish philosophers would agree that every predicate attributed to God is part of an equivocal expression that affirms an absolute moral ideal for human behavior. Furthermore, Cohen's identification of theology and ethics is well rooted in this classical tradition of Jewish philosophy, whose clearest expression is the philosophy of Gersonides. The sole remaining difference between Maimonides and Gersonides has been reduced to just how little we in fact know about God. According to Maimonides, we know something about ethics but absolutely nothing about God; according to Gersonides, moral and theological statements mutually entail each other, so that the very moral commandments we do know are in themselves knowledge of God. In affirming that God is F we affirm that God is F in a primary, absolute way which functions for human behavior as an ideal. Thus, we can differentiate between how we and God know, and affirm that God's way of knowing is superior as an ideal that we, in fulfilling the moral obligation to gain knowledge, constantly attempt to approximate.

Gersonides' conviction—that to gain knowledge is in itself an act of religious devotion that also is inherently moral—contributed much to the passion for learning that came to dominate Jewish life in European society. In this sense Gersonides' own life and thought, like that of his remote disciple, Baruch Spinoza, made a significant contribution to the kind of milieu that produced in a latter period the Freuds, Durkheims, and Einsteins of contemporary Western civilization.

A CHART OF MAJOR INFLUENCES IN THE HISTORY OF WESTERN PHILOSOPHY

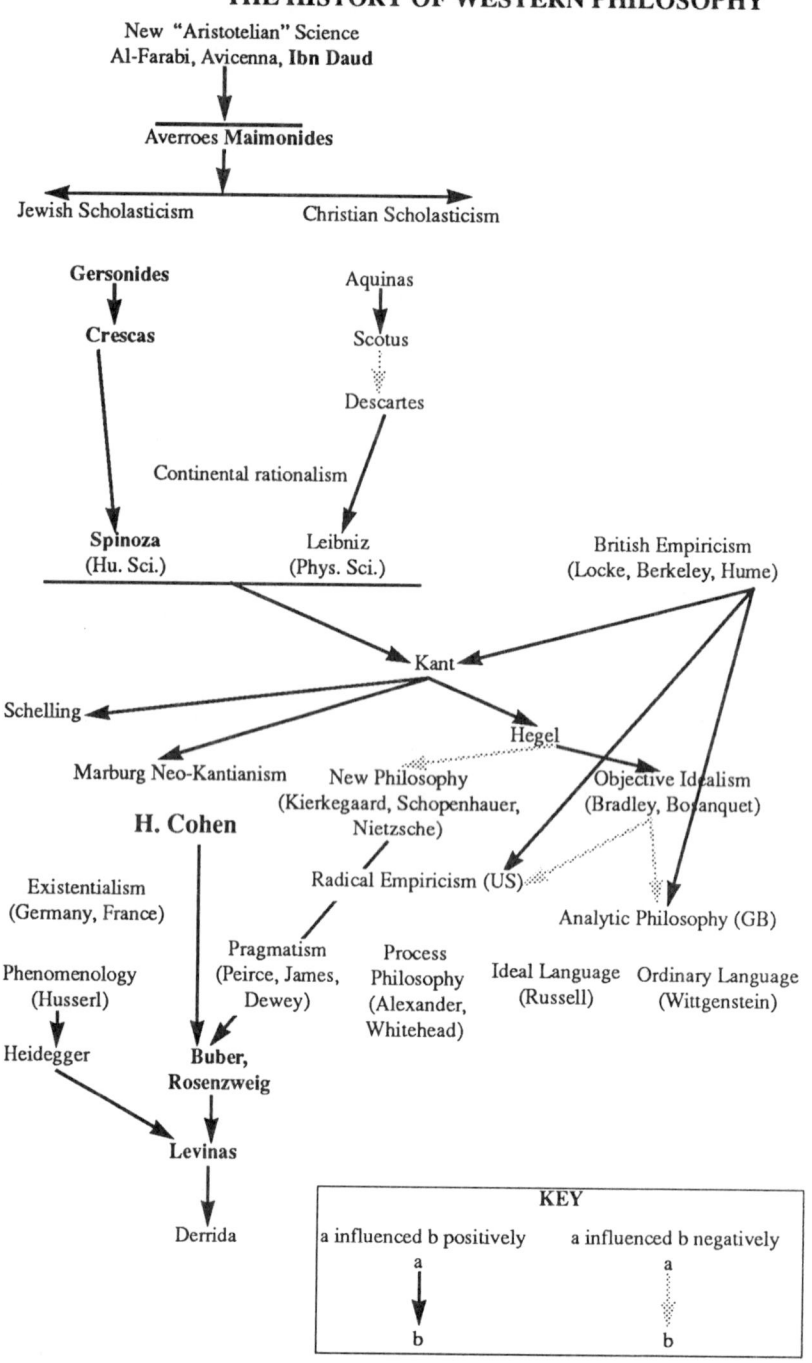

New "Aristotelian" Science
Al-Farabi, Avicenna, **Ibn Daud**

↓

Averroes **Maimonides**

Jewish Scholasticism ← → Christian Scholasticism

Gersonides　　　　　Aquinas

Crescas　　　　　　Scotus
⋮
Descartes

Continental rationalism

Spinoza　　　　Leibniz　　　　　British Empiricism
(Hu. Sci.)　　　　(Phys. Sci.)　　　(Locke, Berkeley, Hume)

Kant

Schelling ←　　　　　　　　　　　Hegel

Marburg Neo-Kantianism　New Philosophy　　Objective Idealism
H. Cohen　　　　　　(Kierkegaard, Schopenhauer,　(Bradley, Bosanquet)
　　　　　　　　　　　Nietzsche)

Existentialism　　　Radical Empiricism (US)
(Germany, France)　　　　　　　　　　　Analytic Philosophy (GB)

　　　　　　Pragmatism　Process
Phenomenology　(Peirce, James,　Philosophy　Ideal Language　Ordinary Language
(Husserl)　　Dewey)　　(Alexander,　(Russell)　　(Wittgenstein)
　　　　　　　　　　　Whitehead)

Heidegger　　　　　**Buber,**
　　　　　　　　Rosenzweig

　　　　　Levinas

　　　　　Derrida

KEY	
a influenced b positively	a influenced b negatively
a ↓ b	a ⋮ b

116

1. Translated into English with a commentary by Norbert M. Samuelson and Gershon Weiss (Cranbury, N.J., 1986).

2. Colette Sirat, in her *A History of Jewish Philosophy in the Middle Ages* (Cambridge, 1985), 308, summarizes the current state of research into the intellectual sources of Gersonides' thought in Western religious philosophy.

3. Specifically on the Maimonidean controversy, see J. Sarachek, *Faith and Reason: The Conflict over the Rationalism of Maimonides* (New York, 1935); D. J. Silver, *Maimonidean Criticism and the Maimonidean Controversy* (Leyden, 1965); and I. Twersky, *Rabad of Posquieres, a Twelfth Century Talmudist* (Cambridge, Mass., 1962). In this context reference should also be made to Byron Sherwin's discussion (in *Mystical Theology and Social Dissent* [Oxford, 1982], 60, 68 and 181) of Rabbi Loew's opposition to studying Gersonides.

4. See Joseph Dan, *Jewish Mysticism and Jewish Ethics* (Philadelphia, 1986). Dan points out that some of the more important communal rabbinic leaders participating in the dispute were in fact Kabbalists, whose motivation for opposing the study of Aristotelian science involved both practical considerations of how too much intellectual sophistication might weaken Jews' resolve to oppose external Christian threats, and a partisan defense of their own commitment to a mystical mode of knowledge beyond what is accessible through natural reason.

5. Cf. D. Ruderman, *The World of a Renaissance Jew: The Life and Thought of Abraham ben Mordecai Farissol* (Cincinnati, 1981).

6. I will not deal here with the details of Gersonides' life. They can be found outlined in Norbert M. Samuelson, *Gersonides on God's Knowledge* (Toronto, 1977), 2-4, and my essay, "Medieval Jewish Philosophy," in *Back to the Sources: Reading the Classic Jewish Texts*, ed. Barry W. Holtz (New York, 1984), 279ff.

7. Henceforth referred to as *The Wars*.

8. At present I am composing a manuscript that deals with the concept of creation out of the sources of Judaism. In terms of rabbinic thought, Gersonides' discussion of creation in Book 6 of *The Wars*, as well as his commentary on the first chapter of Genesis, constitutes the most original and detailed account of this dogma in the Jewish classics. In terms of contemporary Jewish philosophy, the most extensive discussion of creation is to be found in the second book of the second part of Franz Rosenzweig's *The Star of Redemption*. As in the case of divine attributes, there also is a direct historical line between Gersonides' analysis of the divine origin of the universe and Rosenzweig's significantly unique theology of creation.

9. I believe that the issue is an important one, but I have as yet nothing to contribute to this part of the discussion of theology. If I could find an easy way to avoid masculine references I would do so, but I cannot. The use of the feminine does not seem to me to be preferable, and the use of the plural with reference to God clearly is worse. Similarly, to say "it" rather than "he" or "she" or "him" or "her" is worse, since the usage implies that God is not a person. In any case, the problem is the limitation of the English language that provides no genderless term to refer to a person. No serious religious thinker believes that gender is appropriate with respect to God.

10. In this context it is of interest to note that whereas Buber's colleague Franz Rosenzweig focused his attention primarily on creation, revelation and redemption (redemption expressing how man relates to the world, while creation and revelation express God's relationship respectively to the world and man), and Buber dealt extensively with redemption and revelation, Buber said nothing about creation. Creation

has to do with how God relates to the world of objects, what in Buber's language are instances of the I-It relationship; but Buber's deity is always Thou, i.e., an entity who in principle does not and cannot relate to objects. Consequently, in the language adopted for this lecture, Buber clearly dissociated *Elohim* from *Adonai* and only affirmed faith in *Adonai*.

11. The answer to this question depends on the developed doctrine of revelation.

12. Cf. Norbert M. Samuelson, "That the God of the Philosophers is not the God of Abraham, Isaac and Jacob," *Harvard Theological Review* 65 (1972): 1-27.

13. On Einstein's model, space has four dimensions—length, width, depth and time. More contemporary physical theories that attempt to reconcile Newtonian physics with quantum mechanics project mathematical models that involve many more dimensions than four.

14. Cf. Norbert M. Samuelson, "On Proving God's Existence," *Judaism* 16 (1967): 21-36.

15. "Graded predicates" are classes of predicates where individuals who exemplify them are subject to comparative ratings in terms of perfection such that if P and Q are different graded predicates, a is P and b is Q, than either a in virtue of P is greater than b in virtue of Q or b in virtue of Q is greater than a in virtue of P. An example of a class of graded predicates is bowling averages. If John has a 175 bowling average and Mary has a 215 bowling average, then Mary is a better or greater bowler than John. Classes of predicates where this rule does not apply are "nongraded."

"Exclusion predicates" are classes of predicates where the members of the class are so related that it is not possible that any individual who exemplifies one member can exemplify every member of that class. For example, if something is blue all over, then it cannot be red, orange, or any other color complement of blue all over. Classes of predicates where this rule does not apply are "nonexclusion."

16. Diesendruck, Zevi, "The Philosophy of Maimonides," *Central Conference of American Rabbis Yearbook LXV* (1935): 355-368.

Foundations of Jewish Ethics
by
Walter S. Wurzburger

Although classical Jewish literature considers moral conduct one of the essential components of piety, one may question whether there is at all such a subject as Jewish ethics. It is difficult to resist the temptation to declare that there is no such thing as Jewish ethics. For, if it is Jewish, it is not ethics; and if it is ethics, it is not Jewish.

There is an impressive array of serious scholars who contend that Judaism is so radically theocentric and legalistic in orientation that only divine imperatives possess normative validity. Within such a setting, various autonomous moral perceptions cannot be treated as independent sources of moral obligation. For all their divergent approaches, such eminent thinkers or religious authorities as the Chazon Ish,[1] Isaiah Leibowitz,[2] and Marvin Fox[3] agree that, according to traditional conceptions, the Jewish normative system is based exclusively upon halakhah, which is acknowledged as a body of law which, directly or indirectly, derives its authority from divine revelation. As long as the will of God represents the only legitimate normative standard, the term "Jewish ethics" is really a misnomer. For what we designate as ethics is simply halakhah, which derives its authority exclusively from our obligation to submit to the will of God as revealed in his commandments.

But our difficulties with the term "Jewish ethics" would by no means disappear were we to abandon the halakhic stance and adopt the position of a number of liberal Jewish thinkers, who, in the attempt to cast Judaism in the mold of Kantian categories, stripped it of all features that could not be fitted into the Procrustean bed of ethical monotheism. In their view, the promptings of the autonomous human conscience constitute the ultimate court of appeals for all normative issues. As is well known, Kant went so far as to brand as immoral Abraham's readiness to obey God's command to sacrifice his son as a burnt-offering. He should have realized, so Kant argues, that a benevolent God could not possibly have commanded the killing of an innocent person. It was inconceivable that a perfectly moral being such as God would issue commandments which violate the categorical imperative. In the Kantian view, murder would remain murder even if mandated by God. The fact that it would have been explicitly commanded by God would have no bearing upon its morality, since all rational agents, including God, are subject to universally applicable criteria of ethical propriety. Hence, whatever is perceived as immoral by human reason could not possibly have been commanded by God.

It follows from these premises that we can accept as revealed commands of God only what conforms to our own ethical standards. This explains classical Reform Judaism's rejection of all and sundry ritual practices which cannot be shown to contribute to the enhancement of our moral life. Mere submission to a divine command without subjecting it to the scrutiny of the autonomous human conscience was stigmatized by a leading Reform thinker as *Kadavergehorseim* (the obedience of a dead animal), unworthy of a rational being.

But even the adoption of a Kantian approach, which essentially reduces religion to a handmaiden of ethics, would not enable us to speak of a Jewish ethics. If ethics is totally grounded in rationality and is so dependent upon universalizability that it must be divested of all empirical elements, then a Jewish ethics is no more possible than a Jewish mathematics. In the Kantian scheme, particular historic factors cannot have any bearing upon moral considerations. Hence Jewishness must be totally irrelevant to the validity of an ethical approach.

It is highly revealing that Hermann Cohen, one of the foremost exponents of Kant, entitled his exposition of Judaism "The Religion of Reason—Out of the Sources of Judaism." For Cohen, Judaism is merely the source of concepts, ideas and ideals, which enjoy universal applicability and validity. Within the framework of Cohen's pan-ethicism, there is no place for the unique and particular reflecting historic contingencies. In the final analysis, the Jewishness of an ideal or norm does not affect its validity. In other words, there is no Jewish ethics; only a universal ethics out of the sources of Judaism.

Yet, for all our difficulties with the conception of a distinct Jewish ethics, there is a widely and persistently held belief that there is something uniquely Jewish about Jewish ethics. Although Ahad Ha-Am was unable to realize his ambition to demonstrate how the Jewish ethical system differed from those of other cultures or nations, he tenaciously clung to his conviction that the national Jewish spirit manifested itself in a unique approach to ethics. Similarly, Nietzsche was so obsessed with what he considered the debilitating impact of Jewish moral conceptions that he unleashed tirades against what he dubbed "Jewish slave morality," which allegedly had corrupted Western civilization by sapping its vigor and vitality.

While it may not be possible to reconcile the conception of a Jewish ethics with a radical Kantian approach that treats autonomy as the hallmark of morality, it still may be feasible to formulate Jewish conceptions of ethics which are compatible with the acknowledgment of the primacy of a divinely revealed legal system (the halakhah) as the ultimate normative authority. The fact that numerous moral prescriptions are perceived as divine imperatives by no means prevents us from acknowledging them also as moral norms. In this regard, G. E. Moore has pointed out that even for the theist the meaning of the term "good" is not identical with "being commanded by God."[4] It should be borne in mind that numerous medieval Jewish thinkers distinguished between commandments whose moral goodness was recognizable and those which were obeyed solely because they were divine imperatives. Were the property "goodness" translatable into "being commanded by God," one could obviously no longer make this distinction, since the *hukim* (ritual laws for which there was no obvious rational justification) derive their very authority from their being commanded by God.[5]

To be sure, since God is not merely the supreme power but also a morally perfect being, his commandments must be moral. Hence, obedience to his commands is a moral requirement. This being the case, we need not invoke the Kierkegaardian "suspension of the ethical" as justification for Abraham's response to the divine command to offer Isaac as a sacrifice to God. We have every right to claim that Abraham was not merely a "knight of faith," but a knight of morality as well, inasmuch as he was prepared to set aside all considerations of natural sentiments and inclinations in order to fulfill his supreme moral duty—i.e., to obey the highest possible moral authority. As long as he was certain that the command to sacrifice his son truly emanated from God, he was morally and not merely religiously obligated to abide by this divine imperative.[6] It is only because Kierkegaard weighed Abraham's conduct on the scales of Kantian notions of morality that he was unable to provide any kind of ethical justification for the actions of an Abraham. This left him no alternative but to base his defense of Abraham upon the claim that the "suspension of the ethical" represents the highest level of religious loyalty.

It is one thing to assert that all divine imperatives are moral, and another to claim that only what is commanded by a divine imperative can be morally good. Since we do not equate the property "goodness" with the property "commanded by God," the fact that we may regard a certain action as morally desirable in itself constitutes a normative consideration. There is nothing to prevent a theist who regards the will of God as the supreme normative criterion from maintaining that in the absence of conflict with a revealed divine norm, we ought to do or strive to be whatever is perceived to be morally desirable. There is no need to deprive purely moral rules of normative significance. As Yehezkel Kaufmann[7] has pointed out, covenantal morality does not abolish natural morality, but supplements it and supplies it with religious motives and sanctions. Numerous traditional Jewish thinkers dwelt upon the importance of *derekh eretz*, which they defined as commonly accepted notions of morality reflecting utilitarian considerations. In keeping with this interpretation, the rabbinic adage *"derekh eretz* precedes Torah" amounts to an endorsement of a utilitarian morality, which is deemed indispensable to the proper functioning of society.[8]

To be sure, this does not imply that the ethical domain must be acknowledged as an independent normative authority. One could plausibly maintain that a moral imperative automatically becomes also a religious imperative. This is as a matter of fact the position of Nahmanides, who noted that the Torah commands, "Thou shalt do what is right and good" in addition to numerous specific moral prescriptions and norms. In his view, the latter general principle is needed to insure that whatever is perceived as falling within the category of the right and the good is automatically accorded the status of a religious imperative.[9]

Be that as it may, there is absolutely no justification for the canard that Jewish ethics is so legalistic and focuses so exclusively upon narrow, formal requirements that it becomes completely blind to considerations of ethical sensitivity. Jewish ethics, while grounded in law, is not merely an ethics of obedience to specific moral rules but also an ethics of responsibility,[10] which mandates a pattern of conduct reflecting the awareness that all human beings bear the image of God. According to Ben Azzai, the verse "This is the book of the generations of man: when God created man, he created him in his image" constitutes the most fundamental passage of the entire Torah.[11] That such a preeminent position is assigned to this particular verse demonstrates that the belief in the irreducible dignity and sanctity of creatures bearing the divine image plays a pivotal role in the Jewish religio-ethical system.

A cogent argument is advanced by the fifteenth-century Jewish philosopher Joseph Albo[12] in support of the thesis that the area of what is religiously prescribed or recommended must extend beyond the domain of what is the subject of specific legislation of the Torah. After all, the finite number of specific regulations contained in the Torah could not possibly cover all the contingencies arising from ever-changing socio-political and economic conditions. Hence in matters not concretely spelled out in the Torah, we must rely on our own moral perceptions for guidance as to how we can best obey the divine imperative of doing what is right and good. To be sure, these moral perceptions, in turn, should reflect the value system underlying the various particular norms of the Torah. It is expected that as the result of exposure to specific religio-ethical norms, we gradually develop the capacity to intuit theonomous moral requirements that extend beyond the range of the explicitly stated specific norms of the Torah.[13]

It must, however, be realized that the acceptance of the authority and validity of moral intuitions which extend beyond the confines of heteronomous laws in no way entails the acknowledgment of the basic premises of autonomous morality, which looks upon the human self as the ultimate source of moral obligation. In the words of the prophet Micah, "to do justice and to love mercy" is a response to "what God demands of thee"—not a self-imposed duty. Anyone familiar with the history of Jewish ideas is aware that, though apprehended by the human intellect, Bahya's "duties of the heart" or Saadia's "rational commandments" derive their authority not from the autonomous human self but from their status as divine imperatives disclosed by reason. In the telling formation of Menachem Meiri,[14] human beings must be treated with the reverence due to a Torah scroll, because they are endowed with the capacity for discerning with their own minds obligations which are not explicitly stated in the Torah. In a similar vein, Samson Raphael Hirsch[15] refers to an "inner revelation" of God which supplements the "outer revelation" of Sinai. It is through this "inner revelation"—the voice of conscience and reason—that God speaks to us and provides us with moral instruction in the course of the historic process. When moral imperatives are regarded as divine imperatives, it becomes readily understandable why the feature of overridingness distinguishes moral values as opposed to aesthetic or intellectual values. In point of fact, what is perceived as an obligation to our fellow human beings automatically points to an obligation to God. As Emil Fackenheim put it so succinctly, Jewish morality is a three-term morality.[16] Ethics is not an independent sphere but an integral part of the quest for holiness. Hence, ideally, ethical conduct should be inspired by the desire to serve God and to imitate his ways.

Since God represents the supreme moral authority, his imperatives must not be subjected to moral scrutiny. To be sure, we are supposed to interpret his commands in the light of our rational understanding. But obedience to divine imperatives must not be made contingent upon their conformity to our notions of moral propriety. The explicitly revealed will of God must reign supreme. Moral considerations are invoked only in case of doubt concerning the meaning of a divinely revealed norm. It was taken for granted that divine norms must be interpreted in accordance with the principle that Torah reflects the "ways of pleasantness" and the "ways of peace."[17]

It is one thing to adopt this approach as a hermeneutic device for the purpose of determining the meaning of Torah, and another to treat moral perceptions as an independent source of authority. It must be realized that Jewish morality is theocentric not only because divine imperatives, whether obtained through reason or revelation, constitute the ultimate source of authority for its norms, but also because Jewish moral notions originate in specific divine laws governing inter-personal relations such as prohibitions against murder, incest, theft, etc. As Nahmanides pointed out, the meaning of a general principle such as "to do what is right and good" can be grasped only through inductive intuition from a fairly large number of particular instances exemplifying the general principle. Obviously, there is considerably less risk of reading our own subjective preferences into specific laws—e.g., the obligation to place a fence around the roof—than into such broad and general principles as doing the right and the good.

The primacy assigned to specific legal norms also accounts for the unabashedly pluralistic orientation of Jewish ethics. This differs sharply from the bias towards monism that characterizes the bulk of contemporary ethical systems, which seek to justify all moral rules in terms of single principles such as rationality, utility or conformity to human nature. But Judaism eschews all such reductionist efforts. It is prepared to accommodate the requirements of a host of diverse divine imperatives, irrespective of whether or not they are perceived as being compatible with other general principles.

Given the pluralistic nature of Jewish ethics and its potential for clashes between conflicting norms and rules, casuistry—the analysis of the range of applicability of specific moral rules—emerges as one of the key concerns of Jewish ethical thought. In dealing with ethical dilemmas, the specific features of a given existential situation must be examined before informed judgments can be made. This is, of course, the very antithesis of the Kantian approach to ethics, which because of its preoccupation with universalizability insisted upon the utter irrelevance of the unique empirical factors characterizing a given situation. For Kant morality was categorical. History played no role. All that mattered was conformity to an abstract, formal principle. But Jewish morality takes seriously the moral requirements arising from the contingencies of the particular historic situation, be they obligations incurred to a benefactor, to one's family or, for that matter, duties to respond to the special needs of individuals, such as when Hillel offered his services as a footman to an individual who could no longer afford to live in the style to which he was accustomed. From a Jewish perspective, members of our own community have a far greater claim to our benevolence than individuals with whom we have no contact. In rabbinic parlance, the poor of your own city take precedence over the poor of another city.[18] It therefore follows that when competing demands are made upon our resources, we cannot simply determine priorities by computing the maximal utility to mankind. A thousand dollars sent to Africa to provide relief from famine would probably do more good than a thousand dollars spent on the education of my child. But a father must not ignore his specific parental responsibilities. Concern for the good of humanity must be balanced against the institutional responsibilities incurred by becoming a father.

Ahad Ha-Am completely misunderstood the basic thrust of Jewish ethics when he adduced Hillel's negative formulation of the Golden Rule as evidence that Jewish ethics was such a purely formal system that it was concerned only with abstract justice and totally indifferent to considerations involving sentiments such as love, compassion, etc.[19] He conveniently ignored that the performance of acts of benevolence as well as the cultivation of various sentiments such as compassion, sympathy and charity are mandated by Jewish tradition.

Since Jewish morality is responsive to the requirements arising from the unique features of a given existential situation, it is a far cry from the kind of ethics which was denounced by Nietzsche as *Fernstenliebe* (love of the distant). While some Christian moralists may contend that "Love thy neighbor as thyself" implies that, ideally, in matters involving concern for others one should not discriminate between total strangers and members of one's own family, Jewish morality emphasizes that the nature and scope of our moral obligations is affected by historic factors. We cannot love everyone equally. As a matter of fact, according to Judaism, our own life takes precedence over the lives of others. But it is our duty to show every individual the kind of love which is appropriate in the light of the conditions characterizing a particular relationship. To be sure, Judaism rejects the Aristotelian notion that altruism is mandated only vis-à-vis friends. But Jewish morality would agree that bonds of friendship give rise to special obligations which go beyond those due to total strangers.

Inasmuch as a host of cultural and historic elements go into the formation of ethical situations, moral judgments cannot be reduced to simple formal rules. Moreover, moral dilemmas frequently are due to the fact that we do not have at our disposal any formal rule enabling us to assign relative weights to conflicting obligations and competing values. In such cases we have no alternative to reliance upon intuitive perceptions in order to determine the moral requirements of a given existential situation. But there always remains a serious question as to the reliability of such intuitions, which are purely subjective and utterly devoid of any objective validity.

It is for this reason that traditional Jewish conceptions of ethics emphasize the need for guidance obtained through exposure to concrete models of ethical propriety. Since ethical ambiguities cannot be resolved through recourse to canons of formal reasoning, it is essential that we develop our capabilities for ethical judgment by imitation of appropriate role models. This may account for the fact that the Talmud ranks personal contact with scholars above formal study.[20] It is highly revealing that Maimonides, in the section of his Code dealing with the cultivation of virtues,[21] reinterprets in accordance with Jewish needs the Aristotelian doctrine that only the expert in practical wisdom is equipped to provide guidance on matters of ethics. In the Maimonidean scheme, it is only through close association with the *talmid hakham* (Torah scholar) and the careful observation of his conduct that one can obtain an intuitive grasp of what constitutes desirable traits of character—i.e., the proper balance between the extremes that ought to be eschewed.[22] That ethical conduct ultimately presupposes concrete exemplars was also stressed by Rabbi Naftali Tzvi Yehudah Berlin, who contended that the Book of Genesis was included in the Torah because the stories describing the conduct of the Patriarchs were intended to provide ethical role models.[23] Implicit in this view is the belief that the legal part of the Torah would not have sufficed for proper moral guidance. Notwithstanding the fact that the Law constitutes the very foundation of Jewish ethics, these "stories" were indispensable, if the Torah was to provide adequate direction for ethical decision-making, especially with respect to intricate and complex moral issues.

However important the role intuitions play in the realm of act-morality, they assume an even more pivotal role in the sphere of agent-morality. Contrary to the stereotypes associated with Jewish legalism, "agent morality" or "virtue-ethics" is unquestionably a vital component of Jewish ethics. *Sifrei* (Deuteronomy, "*Ekev*," 49) interprets the commandment "Thou shalt walk in his ways" as an imperative to cultivate moral dispositions. Maimonides adopts this approach and devotes an entire section of his Code to virtue-ethics.[24] For that matter, his *Guide of the Perplexed* reaches its grand finale in the kind of *imitatio Dei* which is attained through cultivation of moral dispositions. Moreover, already in one of his earliest works, the *Commentary on the Mishnah*,[25] Maimonides points out that in the ethical sphere performance of the right action alone is totally inadequate. Unless moral actions are the external manifestations of a truly moral personality, one falls considerably short of the moral ideal. Our goal should be the performance of moral actions which are not merely motivated by a sense of duty, but also express the sentiments, inclinations or the very nature of the moral agent.

The centrality of virtue-ethics in the Maimonidean scheme can also be discerned in his treatment of supererogatory conduct. Whereas Nahmanides viewed supererogatory conduct as a para-legal requirement, Maimonides assigned it to the sphere of the "ethics of the pious," which in his scheme presupposes the cultivation of the higher levels of ethical sensitivity through both moral conditioning and intellectual perfection.[26]

It therefore can readily be seen that conformity to the law is treated within Judaism as merely a necessary but not a sufficient condition of morality. The creation of a truly moral personality represents a never-ending task. It is through study and observance of the Law, exposure to the Jewish ethos through living models as well as through the "stories" of the aggadah that we are expected to gradually develop ever higher levels of ethico-religious sensitivity.

But while we must strive for ever loftier rungs of ethical perfection, we must be wary of the pitfalls of a utopian, Messianic ethics. We live in an unredeemed world. It is the height of absurdity to apply to such a world the kind of rules and standards which would be appropriate for a society in which all degradation and violence has been overcome. With all our love of peace, we must categorically reject pacifism. Non-resistance to evil is an unconscionable moral wrong. Perpetration of violence cannot be condoned. We are not merely obligated to resist aggression by force whenever necessary to assist other innocent victims, but we are duty bound to resist aggression even for the protection of our own lives. Here Judaism parts company with the pacifistic streak of Christianity. Judaism rejects the notion that a saint will refuse to resort to force for the sake of self-protection. Judaism is more realistic. It maintains that in our unredeemed world, we must choose the lesser evil (i.e., the killing of an aggressor) over the greater evil (i.e., permitting ourselves to be killed by an aggressor). There are no perfect solutions for an imperfect world. Although we abhor violence, it is our task to conduct ourselves in the here and now, not in accordance with standards appropriate for an ideal Messianic society, but rather in accordance with the requirements of the real world, while hoping that our moral actions may help pave the way for the arrival of the Messiah.[27]

In grappling with the numerous ethical ambiguities and dilemmas we encounter, we must reconcile ourselves to the fact that the moral enterprise is too complex to operate by simplistic rules. The fact that we acknowledge absolute principles in no way dispenses with the need to fall back upon intuition to determine the moral requirements of a given situation. There is constant need for re-assessment and re-evaluation in the light of evolving historic realities and changing ethical sensitivities. In other words, Jewish ethics is dynamic rather than static. As Hillel expressed it to the prospective candidate for conversion, the ongoing quest for the ethical life demands that one "Go forth and study."

1. *Sefer Chazon Ish*, ed. S. Greineman (Jerusalem, 1954), 21-43.
2. Isaiah Leibowitz, *Torah U'Mitzvot Bazeman Hazeh* (Tel Aviv, 1954).
3. Marvin Fox, "Reflections on the Foundations of Jewish Ethics and Their Relation to Public Policy," *Selected Papers*, Society of Christian Ethics, Twenty-First Annual Meeting, 1980, 23-62.
4. G. E. Moore, *Principia Ethica* (Cambridge, 1966).
5. See Aharon Lichtenstein's invaluable discussion of this and other related issues in his essay, "Does Jewish Tradition Recognize an Ethic Independent of Halakha?" in *Modern Jewish Ethics*, ed. Marvin Fox (Columbus, Ohio, 1975), 62-88.
6. See Philip L. Quinn, *Divine Commandments and Moral Requirements* (Oxford, 1978), 96-105. Especially significant is the treatment of this issue in Emil L. Fackenheim, *Encounters Between Judaism and Modern Philosophy* (New York, 1973), 33-37.
7. Yehezkel Kaufmann, *The Religion of Israel*, translated and abridged by Moshe Greenberg (New York, 1960), 233-34 and 327-29.
8. See Judah Loew, *Netivot Olam*, "Netiv Derekh Eretz."
9. Nahmanides, *Commentary to the Torah* to Deut. 6:18.
10. For a more thorough treatment of this subject, refer to my "Covenantal Imperatives," in *Samuel K. Mirsky Memorial Volume* (New York, 1970), 3-12. See also my essay "Law as the Basis of a Moral Society," *Tradition* 19, no. 1 (Spring 1981): 42-54.
11. *Y. Nedarim* 9:4.
12. Joseph Albo, *Sefer ha-Ikkarim* 3:23.
13. That the enactment of new ordinances in response to newly emerging conditions was a corollary of the commandment "to do what is right and good" was pointed out by Vidal Yom Tov of Tolosa, *Maggid Mishneh* to Maimonides' *Mishneh Torah*, "Hilkhot Shekhenim," 14:4.
14. Meiri *ad* Shabbat 105b.
15. Samson Raphael Hirsch, *Horeb*, trans. Dayan Dr. I. Grunfeld, "Introduction," 91.
16. See Emil L. Fackenheim, op. cit., and his essay, "The Revealed Morality of Judaism and Modern Thought," in his *Quest for Past and Future* (Bloomington, Indiana, 1968), 204-228.
17. An excellent collection of the source material can be found in the *Encyclopedia Talmudit*, 7: 712-723.
18. Baba Metzia 71b.
19. Ahad Ha-Am, "Judaism and the Gospels," in *Nationalism and Jewish Ethics: Basic Writings of Ahad Ha'am*, edited and introduced by Hans Kohn (New York, 1962), 301-302.
20. Berakhot 7b.
21. "Hilkhot Deot."
22. Ibid., 6:2
23. Naftali Zvi Yehudah Berlin, *Ha'amek Davar*, Introduction to Genesis.
24. See my discussion of this issue in my "Law as the Basis of a Moral Society," op. cit., 49-51.
25. *Commentary to the Mishnah*, Introduction to Abot, chapter 6.
26. I have dealt more extensively with the implications of the differences between Maimonides' and Nahmanides' conceptions of supererogation in my previously cited essay, "Law as the Basis of a Moral Society."

27. See also my discussion of Messianism in "The Maimonidean Matrix of Rabbi Joseph B. Soloveitchik's Two-Tiered Ethics," in *Through the Sound of Many Voices*, ed. Jonathan V. Plaut (Toronto, 1982), 181-182.